"This is one of the best books on apologetics I've read in years: an accessible and learned presentation of the necessary place of the imagination in a robust defense and integrated explanation of the Catholic faith. Ordway's insights into the nature of language are especially timely and necessary as Christians seek to communicate and witness in a culture swamped by fevered rhetoric and abuse of words."

— CARL E. OLSON —
Editor of IgnatiusInsight.com and *Catholic World Report*

"Holly Ordway has written a fine book on the art of apologetics—offering a reasoned defense of the faith—that situates it nicely in the still broader mission of evangelization. As a convert herself, Dr. Ordway understands that apologetics is the handmaid of evangelization and that it must appeal to the whole person and the whole world. She writes brightly and bracingly for any mind hungry for reality."

— MARK P. SHEA —
Author of *By What Authority?*

"This book is essential reading for anyone who is concerned with the task of communicating the faith—whether through teaching, catechesis, writing, raising children, creating art, or simply day-to-day evangelization. Dr Ordway examines the problem of the 'meaning gap' we face in today's culture and deftly lays out a proposal for an integrated, 'imaginative apologetics' to overcome it. I have no doubt her readers will come away revived and inspired, as I did."

— Teresa Caldecott —
Managing editor of *Second Spring Journal*

"Holly Ordway unveils a gentle and evocative secret weapon: imagination. If the goal of apologetics is not to win a fight but to woo a heart, then *Apologetics and the Christian Imagination* will be passed from Catholic to Catholic like contraband of war."

— Tyler Blanski —
Author of *When Donkeys Talk: A Quest to Rediscover the Mystery and Wonder of Christianity*

"*Apologetics and the Christian Imagination* is a highly accessible introductory book that I will be recommending often. The key concepts are presented clearly and with helpful analogies. Dr. Ordway's explanation of the interaction of the 'twin faculties' of reason and imagination is particularly enlightening."

— Melissa Travis —
Assistant Professor of Apologetics, Houston Baptist University, author of the Young Defenders series

"Holly Ordway is a living example of what happens when both reason and imagination bring about conversion. Yet too often we divorce the two in evangelism and apologetics. In this essential book she demonstrates why the two should never be separated and how Christians can reclaim the art of appealing to both our head and our heart."

— JUSTIN BRIERLEY —
Host of the Unbelievable? radio show and podcast

SERIES EDITOR: FR. DAVID VINCENT MECONI, S.J.
Fr. David Vincent Meconi, S.J., is a Jesuit priest and professor of theology at Saint Louis University where he also serves as the Director of the Catholic Studies Centre. He is the editor of *Homiletic and Pastoral Review* and has published widely in the areas of Church history and Catholic culture. He holds the pontifical license in Patristics from the University of Innsbruck in Austria, and the D.Phil. in Ecclesiastical History from the University of Oxford.

ABOUT THE SERIES

The great Christian Tradition has always affirmed that the world in which we live is a reflection of its divine source, a place perhaps torn apart by sin but still charged with busy and bustling creatures disclosing the beautiful presence of God. The *Living Faith* series consists of eminent Catholic authors who seek to help Christians navigate their way in this world. How do we understand objective truth in a culture insistent on relativism? How does one evangelize in a world offended when invited to something higher? How do we understand sin and salvation when so many have no real interest in becoming saints? The *Living Faith* series will answer these and numerous other questions Christians have today as they set out not only to live holy lives themselves, but to bring others to the fullness of life in Christ Jesus.

Catholicism and Intelligence
Fr. James V. Schall, S.J.

The Family of God and How Christ Lives In His Church Today
Carl E. Olson

Jesus Christ in Islam and Christianity
Fr. Mitch Pacwa, S.J.

Holiness and Living the Sacramental Life
Fr. Philip-Michael Tangorra

The Joyful Mystery: Notes Toward a Green Thomism
Christopher J. Thompson

Spirituality of the Business World
Michael Naughton

Sanctity and Scripture
Scott Hahn

The Adventure of Christianity
Daniel Keating

Catholic and at College
Anne Carson Daly

*Living Grace & Deadly Sin: A Guide to Getting Our
Souls Straight*
Fr. David Vincent Meconi, S.J.

APOLOGETICS
and the
CHRISTIAN
IMAGINATION

APOLOGETICS
and the
CHRISTIAN IMAGINATION

An Integrated Approach to Defending the Faith

HOLLY ORDWAY

Steubenville, Ohio
www.emmausroad.org

Emmaus Road Publishing
1468 Parkview Circle
Steubenville, Ohio 43952

Library of Congress Cataloging-in-Publication Data
Names: Ordway, Holly, author.
Title: Apologetics and the Christian imagination: an integrated approach to
defending the faith / Holly Ordway.
Description: Steubenville : Emmaus Road Pub., 2017. | Series: Living faith |
  Description based on print version record and CIP data provided by
  publisher; resource not viewed.
Identifiers: LCCN 2017006938 (print) | LCCN 2017012710 (ebook) | ISBN
  9781945125393 (ebook) | ISBN 9781945125386 (hardcover)
Subjects: LCSH: Apologetics. | Imagination--Religious aspects--Christianity.
  | Philosophical theology.
Classification: LCC BT1103 (ebook) | LCC BT1103 .O73 2017 (print) | DDC
  239--dc23
LC record available at https://lccn.loc.gov/2017006938

Cover design and layout by Margaret Ryland
NEED COVER IMAGE ATTRIBUTION

TABLE OF CONTENTS

To Malcolm Guite

CHAPTER ONE

What Is Imaginative Apologetics?

WHAT is the role of the imagination in Christian apologetics? Before we answer that question, we should ask: what is *apologetics* in the first place?

Has anyone ever asked you, "Why do you believe that?" or "How do we know that God is real?" Perhaps you have a friend or family member who has doubts about Christianity—or you've wrestled with doubts yourself. Is your son or daughter headed to college, where he or she will encounter challenges and temptations to abandon the Faith? Do you have colleagues or friends who are hostile to the Church? Have you ever wondered how on earth you can talk to anyone about Christ in the first place?

Responding to these kinds of questions and helping to resolve these doubts is the work of apologetics—and it's relevant in every Christian's life. Despite the name, 'apologetics' doesn't mean apologizing for one's faith; it comes from the Greek word *apologia*, which means 'to make a defense for': in short, to explain why what we believe is true. As St. Peter put it: "Always be ready to make your defense to anyone who demands from you an accounting for the hope that is in you."[1] St. Paul is perhaps the first apologist, explaining to the Athenians on Mars Hill that the intuitions of their pagan religion were clarified and fulfilled in Christ, and reminding the Corinthians that the Resurrection actually happened in history, with eyewitnesses—and that it is the foundation of our Faith.

The Great Commandment tells us to love God with "heart, soul, strength, and mind"[2]—that is, with the whole person: intellect, emotions, will. To be sure, we can love and obey God without knowing much about him (thank God!); the gift of faith is not limited to those who can give explanations for their faith. But if we have the opportunity to learn, we should do so: we are called to child-*like*, trusting faith, not child-*ish*, ignorant faith. After all, anyone who has spent any time around children knows that they are far more inquisitive than most adults. Children by nature want to learn about the world; they fearlessly ask questions, because they trust that their parents and teachers can answer those questions. So, too, with learning about our Faith and sharing what we know. We are all called to evangelize—to share the good news—and also to help people understand that the Gospel really is good news, and that it is *true.*

Apologetics isn't the province just of specialist scholars and scholarly saints, but of ordinary men and women in every walk of life: parents and teachers, lay ministry leaders, priests and pastors, to be sure, but also anyone who has a friend or colleague with doubts, or who wants to be

[1] 1 Peter 3:15.
[2] Mark 12:30; Luke 10:27.

able to invite others to the Faith. Indeed, apologetics is for everyone who wants to develop a stronger faith, to really understand why we believe what we believe, to know Our Lord better and love him more fully. However, this essential work of sharing the Faith, and helping others to grow in it, is increasingly difficult to do in the modern day.

THE POST-CHRISTIAN CONTEXT

We live in what is essentially a post-Christian age. Church attendance has dropped; increasing numbers of people feel comfortable admitting to agnosticism or atheism; every day the media gives evidence of a deep-seated hostility toward Christianity (especially on any topic related to sexual ethics).

Paradoxically, we live in an age of unprecedented information access combined with widespread religious illiteracy. Never has there been more material available on the rational and historical grounds for Christian faith, yet it's ever more mainstream to question even Jesus's existence, let alone his divinity, and *Da Vinci Code*-style conspiracy theories flourish. Access to Holy Scripture is extraordinary—from countless different translations and themed editions of the Bible in every bookstore, to free online search engines for Scripture—but nonetheless many people (including in national media!) regularly make basic errors of fact about what the Bible says (even leaving aside how they interpret it). Books, podcasts, YouTube videos, public lectures, and websites are all readily available for anyone who wants to inform himself on what Christians believe—but we're not seeing widespread, serious engagement with Christian thought or teaching.

Non-believers today know that Christianity is an option. Those who are only nominal Christians or who have walked away from the Church know that they could find out more if they wanted to. Access is not the problem.

The problem is that, all too often, people think they already know what Christianity is—and they don't particularly want to hear any more about it. Many people have only a vague idea of Jesus, one that's frankly not interesting enough to be worth bothering about; for them, Christianity is just one more option on the spiritual menu, and an outdated one at that. Some hold the Faith in contempt as a superstition, or believe Christianity to be a dangerous ideology that threatens what they hold dear. Many others simply don't care very much. They may be content to acknowledge Jesus's cultural or historical significance, or admire him as a distant, inspirational figure, while remaining indifferent to his Church. Still others consider the Faith to be a private matter, an opinion or personal taste, entirely subjective and certainly entirely separate from the serious business of education, government, and personal fulfillment.

The reality is that many people just aren't listening the way we hope they're listening when we share the Gospel.

But then, why should people listen to us? There are many competing claims on their attention. Furthermore, the orthodox Christian position, and especially Catholic teaching, is often tarred with claims of ignorance, intolerance, and bigotry; without a compelling reason to approach, many people will prudently keep their distance. And they won't feel that they're missing out, because to them, apologetics and evangelization are just so much meaningless noise—irrelevant or disagreeable depending on their point of view, but in any case, nothing to think about seriously.

What are we to do? The very people who most need to hear the truth are often the ones most resistant to listening to us!

Here we see the need for a new approach—or rather, the return to an older, more integrated approach to apologetics. Evangelization means, in the most basic sense, saying like St. Andrew, St. Philip, or the Samaritan woman, "I have found the Lord; come with me, come and see for yourself."[3] Always, though, people need a motive to answer that call to "come and see." This motive might be simple curiosity. It might be the recognition of need, or the awakening of a longing for the divine. It might be respect or affection for the person who extends the invitation. But in any case, and in every case, a connection is necessary: some sort of imaginative engagement with the idea, or at least the possibility, that there might be something worth seeing.

What might that imaginative engagement look like in practice? Let me tell you two stories.

THE FIRST STORY: C. S. LEWIS

The first story is about someone you probably know, at least by name. C. S. Lewis—the most famous and influential popular apologist of the twentieth century—was not always a Christian. He came to faith as an adult—and the

---

[3] John 1:40–41, 45–46; 4:28–29.

imagination played a critical role in his conversion as well as in his subsequent writing.

In his autobiography, *Surprised by Joy*, Lewis notes that as a young man, he was profoundly influenced by reading the novel *Phantastes*, by the Christian author George MacDonald. *Phantastes* is a fairy tale, a story that does not mention Christ or the Church or the Bible anywhere in its pages. But it is deeply imbued with the Christian worldview, and conveys what Lewis called the "bright shadow" of what he would later recognize as "Holiness."[4] When he read this book, Lewis had a sense of this bright shadow "coming out of the book into the real world and resting there, transforming all common things and yet itself unchanged."[5] He added that at this point, "my imagination was, in a certain sense, baptized; the rest of me, not unnaturally, took longer."[6] Imaginatively, he had tasted something of transcendence, and gained a glimpse of the Christian vision of the world. Intellectually, he was still a convinced atheist.

Lewis's studies at Oxford University gave him the opportunity to dig more deeply into ultimate questions. He took a double First Class degree in 'Greats' (Classics, Philosophy, and Ancient History) and English and, indeed, taught philosophy as well as English in his early years as an Oxford don. Wrestling with the philosophical questions of the day, with the idea of the Absolute, and with his own experiences of the transcendent, he realized that

---

[4] C. S. Lewis, *Surprised by Joy: The Shape of My Early Life* (Orlando, FL: Harcourt, 1955), 179.

[5] Ibid., 181.

[6] Ibid.

his deepest longings for what he called 'Joy' could only be fulfilled in God. Eventually, as he recounts in *Surprised by Joy*, he "gave in, and admitted that God was God, and knelt and prayed: perhaps, that night, the most dejected and reluctant convert in all England."[7]

However, this was a conversion to Theism, not to Christianity; the God he had acknowledged was not personal. By 1931, Lewis still found himself unable to accept the claims of Christianity. His difficulty at this point was no longer primarily intellectual; for instance, his letters to his friend Arthur Greeves show that he knew the facts about the Christian doctrines of salvation and the atonement. In one letter, attempting to explain how he had finally "passed on from believing in God to definitely believing in Christ—in Christianity"[8]—Lewis says specifically: "What has been holding me back (at any rate for the last year or so) has not been so much a difficulty in believing as a difficulty in knowing what the doctrine *meant*: you can't believe a thing while you are ignorant *what* the thing is."[9] In trying to understand the sacrifice of Christ on the Cross, Lewis kept coming up against something "very mysterious, expressed in those phrases I have so often ridiculed ('propitiation'—'sacrifice'—'the blood of the Lamb')—expressions which I could only interpret

[7] Ibid., 228–29.

[8] C. S. Lewis, letter to Arthur Greeves, Oct. 1, 1931, *Collected Letters vol. I*, ed. Walter Hooper (London: HarperCollins, 2000), 974.

[9] C. S. Lewis, letter to Arthur Greeves, Oct. 18, 1931, *Collected Letters vol. I*, 976. See also *C. S. Lewis: A Biography*, by Roger Lancelyn Green and Walter Hooper, Revised edition (San Diego: Harcourt Brace, 1974).

in senses that seemed to me either silly or shocking."[10]

He was struggling not with missing facts, but with missing *meaning*: he had not been able to grasp the fullness of the idea of Christ's sacrifice. As he explained to Greeves, this difficulty with meaning was what his friends Hugo Dyson and J. R. R. Tolkien helped him with, one day in 1931 as he walked with them through the grounds of Magdalen College, Oxford:

> Now what Dyson and Tolkien showed me was this: that if I met the idea of sacrifice in a Pagan story . . . I liked it very much and was mysteriously moved by it. . . . Now, the story of Christ is simply a true myth: a myth working on us in the same way as the others, but with this tremendous difference that *it really happened*.[11]

He went on to sum up what had occurred: he had realized that the doctrines of Christianity come from the "true myth": "they are translations into our *concepts* and *ideas* of that which God has already expressed in a language more adequate, namely the actual incarnation, crucifixion, and resurrection."[12] Tolkien and Dyson had, in fact, used Lewis's love of myth and mythic stories to help him see the truth of Christianity. When Lewis realized that he could connect his imaginative response to the story, to the factual reality of the Christian claim about the Crucifix-

[10] Ibid.
[11] Ibid., 976–977.
[12] Ibid., 977.

ion and Resurrection, the final barrier to belief fell. He could become a Christian as a whole person, with both his imagination and his reason fully engaged.

THE SECOND STORY: HOLLY ORDWAY

The second story is my own. Like Lewis, I am an adult convert to the Faith. Before my conversion, I was an atheist, and a hostile one, who agreed with the New Atheists that Christianity was not just false, but irrational and harmful.

Philosophical and historical apologetics eventually played an important role in my conversion—the work of scholars such as William Lane Craig and N.T. Wright. I would not have been able to accept Christ if I had not become convinced that Christianity is indeed a rational faith, that it is true, and that the Resurrection is a fact of history. But when I was so firmly an atheist, I found the very idea of faith to be so repellent that I *would not have listened* to the arguments that ultimately convinced me.

However, although I was not interested in Christianity, I had, without knowing it, been experiencing the work of grace through my imagination. As a child and young adult, I read fantasy, fairy tales, and myths, and I especially fell in love with the Chronicles of Narnia and *The Lord of the Rings*. I didn't know that I was encountering God's grace through those books, but in fact I was. Later, I wrote my doctoral dissertation on fantasy novels, and had Tolkien's great essay "On Fairy-stories," with its powerful statement of the *evangelium*, the good news, at the heart of it. Later, I began to teach college literature, and in revisiting classic poetry for my class preparation, I was deeply moved and intrigued by the writings of specifically Christian poets. I had to admit that whatever it was that these authors believed, it was not simplistic or silly. Eventually, I realized that this question of 'faith' was more complex, and more interesting, than I had thought . . . and I decided to learn more.

There were a lot of questions that I needed to ask and have answered before I came to accept Christ, but imagination opened the door. As George MacDonald's novel *Phantastes* baptized C. S. Lewis's imagination, so Lewis, Tolkien, Donne, and Hopkins had baptized mine.

But also like Lewis, I had a two-step conversion. I came to belief in God, but then struggled with the idea of the Incarnation. All the evidence pointed toward the crucifixion and the Resurrection as historical facts, but I found that I was unable to *accept* the idea of Jesus as God Incarnate. I understood the concept, but I couldn't grasp it, even though I knew that it was part of a larger argument that was extremely convincing.

At that point, I turned very deliberately to the Chronicles of Narnia and began re-reading them, because I knew what I needed: I went looking for Aslan, the lion who is the great Christ-figure of the Chronicles. I re-read *The Lion, the Witch and the Wardrobe* and *The Horse and His Boy*, both of which prominently feature Aslan. And through my experience of those stories, my imagination was able to connect with what my reason already knew, and I was able to *grasp*, as a whole person, that it could be true: that God could become Incarnate. And that *imaginative* experience removed the last stumbling block for my acceptance of Christ.

For both C. S. Lewis and myself, imagination and reason were both necessary for conversion. Reason and imagination are twin faculties, both part of human nature—and both given to us by God our Creator!—that, together, allow for a fuller grasp of the truth. Both of them are necessary and valuable. But as we will see, it is the *imagination* that provides the foundation for the exercise of the reason—and the imagination has been sorely neglected in apologetics, evangelization, and catechesis.

APOLOGETICS AND EVANGELIZATION

Here it is worth pausing to make a distinction between 'apologist' and 'evangelist' and, in the process, define the work of the apologist with greater precision. 'Evangelization' (or 'evangelism') is the broader category: sharing the *evangelium*, the good news. Jesus tells the disciples, "Go therefore and make disciples of all nations, baptizing them in the name of the Father and of the Son and of the Holy Spirit"[13]—a command to evangelize. Proclamation of the Gospel, preaching, and calls to repentance and conversion are the primary work of the evangelist. 'Apologetics' is the more specific category, working in two ways: negatively to address challenges to the Faith, resolve doubts, remove obstacles to belief, and dismantle false ideas; and positively to show the truth, coherence, power, and beauty of Christianity.

Apologetics is valuable not only for helping skeptics and those who have fallen away from the Faith, but also for the discipleship and spiritual growth of faithful Christians. Every baptized Christian is called to conversion: a daily, hourly re-orienting of the self to Christ; a renewal

---

[13] Matthew 28:19.

and deepening of commitment; growth in knowledge and love of God. We are assailed by competing claims for our loyalty of heart and mind; we are constantly being tempted, distracted, and confused; we need to be nourished and strengthened in mind, heart, and will.

If we look at the way that conversion is presented in Scripture and the way that it has been worked out in the tradition of the Church, we see more of a process than a single experience. For an adult convert, the process of conversion would include repentance, instruction in the Faith via the catechumenate, baptism, and then ongoing growth in one's life of prayer, devotion, worship, and service.

I would suggest the image of the apologist as a gardener. The 'narrow way' can be blocked by large obstacles such as fallen rocks, which can be rolled aside; it can be overgrown by brambles till the path is barely visible at all, so that pruning and weeding makes the path visible once again; it can be neglected till it's little more than a dusty footpath through a scrubby field, so that tending and beautifying the path, and putting up helpful sign-boards, can make it attractive as a path for befuddled wanderers. The evangelist calls people to the path and teaches them about the journey and the destination; the apologist helps make the journey possible, both at early stages of the process and throughout the Christian's life as he or she grows in knowledge and love of God.

Thus, apologetics is as much needed *within* the Church as without. It helps Christians to strengthen and deepen their own spiritual lives, by showing them how all the teachings of the Church fit together into a deeply meaningful whole; it enables people to recognize heresy and reject it before it does harm (and our modern culture promotes heresy in many subtle forms!); it provides a foundation for understanding the Scriptures and Christian doctrine more fully, and thus for gaining more spiritual and intellectual nourishment from preaching, teaching, and devotional reading. And, of course, apologetics helps Christians to speak about the Faith to others with greater confidence and effectiveness, and thus to strengthen the faith of family and friends as well as to help non-believers encounter Our Lord.

Conversion involves the whole person: the mind, the heart, and most importantly the will. Some obstacles to faith are conceptual or factual; one can't accept Jesus as Lord if one thinks he never existed. Other obstacles are emotional, such as the fear of being rejected by friends and family if one becomes a Christian.[14] Some are obstacles of the will: a refusal to accept the moral obligations that the Christian faith makes evident. Still another kind of obstacle that we find today is compartmentalization: the walls that can be (consciously or unconsciously) set up between the different parts of the human being, so that the Gospel call is heard only in the mind, or only in the emotions, but not in the whole self. The apologist can help to remove these obstacles so that the work of evangelization will bear fruit.

Ultimately, we must trust in the work of the Holy Spirit; neither through reasoned arguments nor beautiful

---

[14] A very well-founded fear in many cases, especially for converts of Muslim backgrounds. See, for instance, Nabeel Qureshi's *Seeking Allah, Finding Jesus*.

art can we *make* someone a Christian. As Michael Ward puts it: "The message will remain folly to the world however wise the medium."[15] Nonetheless we are called to the Great Commission, and charged with giving a reason for our hope. We can clear the way, and point to Christ, as John the Baptist did; we can say "Yes" to the work God asks us to do, as, pre-eminently, Mary does, in bringing her Son into the world, always pointing to him and telling us, "Do whatever he tells you."[16]

As Austin Farrer explains, the work of apologetics does not stand on its own, but rather cultivates an environment in which belief can develop: "Though argument does not create conviction, the lack of it destroys belief. What seems to be proved may not be embraced; but what no one shows the ability to defend is quickly abandoned. Rational argument does not create belief, but it maintains a climate in which belief may flourish."[17] I would add to Farrer's point in this way: we need above all to cultivate an environment in which belief is both *reasonable* and *meaningful*.

When people lack imaginative engagement with the Faith—which may include a deficit of real meaning for the words and ideas that we use, or a failure to see that these ideas are important or interesting—their belief (or potential belief) is not so much destroyed as starved. Ra-

---

[15] Michael Ward, "Escape to Wallaby Wood: C. S. Lewis's Depictions of Conversion," in *C. S. Lewis: Lightbearer in the Shadowlands*, ed. Angus Menuge (Wheaton, IL: Crossway, 1997), 146.

[16] John 2:5.

[17] Austin Farrer, "The Christian Apologist," in *Light on C. S. Lewis*, ed. Jocelyn Gibbs (New York: Harcourt, Brace & World, 1965), 26.

tional argument helps to remove the stones and choking weeds from the field we seek to cultivate, but without imagination the soil is dry and hard and the seeds are easily scorched or blown away. Culturally, we are, as it were, in drought conditions for the sowing of the Word.

Here we turn from considering apologetics, broadly speaking, to the more specific topic of what we will call *imaginative* apologetics. Both reason and imagination are modes of communicating and encountering truth; *imaginative apologetics* seeks to harness the God-given faculty of imagination to work in cooperation with reason, to open a way for the work of the Holy Spirit and guide the will toward a commitment to Christ.

WHAT IS THE FACULTY OF IMAGINATION?

At the most basic level, the imagination is what allows us to conceive in our minds the image of something that is not present: what Tolkien calls "the mental power of image-making."[18] We may not at first realize just how significant this "mental power" really is. In our modern culture, 'imagination' tends to be associated with things that are 'imaginary': entertainment through made-up stories, whether these are a child's fanciful tales or a Hollywood sci-fi blockbuster. Many people consider the imagination to be at best a fanciful extra at best, or a dangerous source of lies and deception at worst.[19] However, this is a sadly

---

[18] J. R. R. Tolkien, "On Fairy-stories," in *Tolkien On Fairy-stories: Expanded edition, with commentary and notes,* ed. Verlyn Flieger and Douglas A. Anderson (London: HarperCollins, 2014), 59.

[19] There is merit to the warning that the imagination can deceive; indeed, it can. But so can reason. Any human faculty can be used for

impoverished and limited view of the imagination.

For Aristotle, and for St. Augustine, St. Thomas Aquinas, St. Bonaventure, and other medieval scholars and theologians, the imagination has a cognitive function: it mediates "between sense and intellect"[20] by conveying "data to the intellect."[21] According to St. Bonaventure, the imagination both stores images for later recall, and also interacts with the intellect by supplying the intellect with sensory data that has been "put into a form that the intellect can act on and use to understand."[22] Imagination is the human faculty that assimilates sensory data into images, upon which the intellect can then act; it is the basis of all reasoned thought as well as all artistic, or what we would call 'imaginative,' exercise.[23] C. S. Lewis, who was first and foremost a scholar of Medieval and Renaissance literature, draws on this more robust understanding of the imagination. Lewis writes that "reason is the natural organ of truth; but imagination is the organ of meaning. Imagination, producing new metaphors or revivifying old, is not the cause of truth, but its condition."[24]

---

good or for evil, and all language can be used to speak either truth or falsehood.

[20] Michelle Karnes, *Imagination, Meditation, and Cognition in the Middle Ages* (Chicago: The University of Chicago Press, 2011), 31.

[21] Ibid., 33.

[22] Ibid., 87.

[23] Notably, the medieval perspective holds that Christ is active in all of our experiences of knowing.

[24] C. S. Lewis, "Bluspels and Flalansferes: A Semantic Nightmare," in *Selected Literary Essays* (Cambridge: Cambridge University Press, 1969), 265.

Thus, imagination is related to reason, and *necessarily* so: not related in the way that the two sides of a coin are related to each other, but related in the way that a building's foundation is related to the structure that is built upon it. Reason is dependent on imagination.

One way of illustrating the necessity of imagination for the use of reason is through an experience that nearly everyone has had. You're looking at a crowd of people, perhaps at an airport or in a party, looking for a friend. You see someone coming toward you—is this your friend? There is a moment when you have the sensory data available to your eyes, but you are unsure of the identification—is this really the person you're looking for, or a stranger?—and then there is a moment when the data resolves into meaning, and you are able to identify the person either as *not* the person you're collecting at the airport, or *yes*, this is your friend. The senses bring the data; the reason makes the identification; the imagination mediates between the two.

In *Poetic Diction*, Owen Barfield argues that "the mind is never aware of an idea until the imagination has been at work on the bare material given by the senses."[25] Not even science is exempt from the necessity of the imagination, because the intellect cannot deal directly with raw perceptions of the world: "Only by imagination . . . can the world be known."[26] In the example of spotting your friend in the midst of a crowd, it is the senses that bring

---

[25] Owen Barfield, *Poetic Diction: A Study in Meaning* (Middletown, CT: Wesleyan University Press, 1973), 26–27.
[26] Ibid., 28.

you the data—clothing, hair, height, movement—and the imagination that converts the data into something meaningful upon which the reason can then act, to perform the mental act of recognition.

When we get intellectual information from reading and listening to others, this data is likewise mediated through the senses: sight and hearing. We can see this from another example: reading. You are reading these words right now: what your eyes see are small black squiggles on a white background, which you must interpret as letters; the letters in groups must be interpreted as words; and the words must be interpreted for their meaning. Until this sensory data has been assimilated, your reason cannot judge whether the meaning of the words is true or false. Perhaps you are listening to an audio version of this book; if so, my example of seeing the letters is not applicable in your case. However, you cannot make the reasoned judgment of whether the example is applicable or not until you have assimilated the audio or visual data and your imagination has rendered it into meaningful words.

In this broad sense, imagination is constantly at work in everyone, whether we realize it or not. It is not possible to have even a minimal grasp of propositional knowledge without the effective working of the faculty of imagination. However, as a robust mode of knowing, imagination has been cut off from reason and neglected as a means of communicating truth. For the past several hundred years, but especially in the twentieth century, Western culture has increasingly accepted a very limited view of the world, in which only the things that can be measured or experimentally verified are considered to be real or true. In this materialist view of the world, reason and imagination have little to do with each other.

The effects of this split between reason and imagination on the meaning of religious language are exacerbated by the rise of cultural illiteracy in Western culture (among Christians as well, unfortunately). In past centuries, preachers, teachers, and apologists could at least count on a basic cultural context that supplied some degree of meaning for religious language. In church, worshippers had the opportunity for imaginative engagement in many different modes, as they would encounter Christian ideas not only in the Scripture readings and in the sermons, but also in stained glass windows, statues, icons, works of art, clerical vestments, gestures (such as genuflections and crossings), and the symbolism of the liturgy. Up until a few decades ago, Christianity was a cultural institution, which meant that most adults had a basic familiarity with Scripture and with the central ideas of Christianity, whether or not they believed. In this context, apologists could count on a certain level of meaning provided by cultural exposure. However, in the twenty-first century, with fragmented communities and a thoroughly secular educational system, even this limited degree of context has in many cases been lost.[27]

The world is flooded with data, and it is fatally easy to be overwhelmed by it; and it may be that the last cry of those drowning in nonsense is "What does it all *mean?*"

---

[27] Evidence for this can be seen in the extent to which Scriptural allusions in literature require explanatory notes in college texts, when the original works, often written for a broader audience than college-educated readers, assumed that the reader would recognize the references.

How can meaning be imaginatively created, and how can it be used by the apologist to draw the seeker toward Christ? Such are the questions we will consider as we go forward.

CONVERSION

A twitch upon the thread, and here I stand,
Pausing at this door. I wish that I
Could look aside, or back away, pretend
I don't see where this threshold leads, deny
The summons and the sudden urgency
That blows away as so much useless chaff
My nonchalant excuses for delay.
I thought I had control, I was in charge,
Until I followed truth, which led me here,
Where I both want and fear to enter in.
I must lay down my arms, that much is clear;
But this is not the end. Here I begin—
For where else could I go if I retreat?
What better victory win than this defeat?

·❖·

CHAPTER TWO

CREATING MEANING

WE are awash in data, awash in claims for and against Christianity—and for and against any number of competing ideologies and lifestyles, ranging from Marxism, gender ideology, and radical feminism to health fads and fashion. One lifetime isn't enough to weigh the merits of each of these; in the meantime, dialogue is often reduced to shouting slogans back and forth (a problem not limited to religious dialogue, to be sure). In the chaotic shopping-mall environment of modern media, the call to "follow Christ" or "repent and be baptized" or even "love God and your neighbor" must compete with "just do it" and "have it your way," and with a million images that wordlessly present the modern gospel of sex, money, fame, and power.

No wonder, then, that Christianity is more often ignored or mocked than thoughtfully discussed. To those who do not know Christ, and unfortunately also to many who do, much 'Christian language' rings empty. Although words like 'grace,' 'sin,' 'heaven,' and 'hell' point to reality, for many listeners they might as well be empty slogans or the equivalent of the user's agreement on an upgrade to your phone's operating system: words that are received without attention, and without a grasp of their meaning. It is this lack of meaning, rather than disagreement with Christian doctrine properly understood, that often presents the most significant barrier to any serious consideration of the Faith.

Michael Ward sums up the problem nicely in his essay "The Good Serves the Better and Both the Best: C. S. Lewis on Imagination and Reason in Apologetics." Ward writes:

> It is no good arguing for 'God' or 'Christ' or for 'the atonement' or even for 'truth' until the apologist has shown, at least at some basic level, that these terms have real meaning. Otherwise they will just be counters in an intellectual game, leaving most readers cold. Likewise, apologetic arguments for the authority of the 'Church' or 'the Bible' or 'experience' or 'reason' itself, must all be imaginatively realized before they can begin to make traction on the reader's reason, let alone on the reader's will.[1]

For instance, the statement "Jesus loves you" may be meaningless to a skeptic on a number of levels. For the Christian, this statement about Our Lord's love is profoundly

---

[1] Michael Ward, "The Good Serves the Better and Both the Best: C. S. Lewis on Imagination and Reason in Apologetics," in *Imaginative Apologetics: Theology, Philosophy, and the Catholic Tradition*, ed. Andrew Davison (Grand Rapids, MI: Baker Academic, 2011), 72.

meaning-*full*; it connects to life-changing insights about hope for eternal life, joy in the present life, and the availability of forgiveness and grace for all who turn and ask. But, as we will explore in a later chapter, it makes a difference whether people *want* this hope, joy, forgiveness, and grace. If they are not interested, or do not find those ideas, in turn, to be meaningful, then all that is represented by "Jesus loves you" is insubstantial and irrelevant.

That's a best-case scenario; at worst, a statement like "Jesus loves you" comes across like the nonsense-language in Lewis Carroll's poem "Jabberwocky."[2] The sentence, while grammatically coherent, makes about as much sense to the atheist as saying "Winston Churchill loves you" or "King Arthur loves you." The skeptic may not believe that Jesus existed at all, but even if he does concede Jesus's historical existence, another question arises: how is it possible for a man who died two thousand years ago to 'love' anyone? An attempt to further explain will likely use terms such as 'the Christ,' 'the Son of God,' and the 'Savior,' but the explanation will fall flat if those terms are also just "counters in an intellectual game."

Likewise, an attempt to talk about the Resurrection can lead to endless rabbit-trails of debating implausible alternatives, but not necessarily because the atheist is convinced by arguments that the disciples experienced group hallucinations, or that they conspired to hide the body and lie about the Resurrection. Rather, the atheist may

---

2 "Twas brillig, and the slithy toves / Did gyre and gimble in the wabe: / All mimsy were the borogoves, / And the mome raths outgrabe." Brilliant as these opening lines are, no one realistically expects to encounter a tove or a mome rath whilst walking in the park.

favor even a highly implausible explanation of the empty tomb, simply because concepts like hallucinations, conspiracies, or even aliens have more meaning for him than 'resurrection from the dead' or 'miracle.'

Even when two people are agreed about the dictionary definition of a word (a not insignificant achievement), still the word may not hold genuine *meaning* for both participants in the conversation. If the word 'resurrection' is an abstraction, an *idea* about something that *might have* happened, rather than the particular details of an event that physically happened to the dead body of a particular man named Jesus on a particular day in history, then the discussion can become pointless without us even realizing it.[3] Even the most convincing historical evidence for the

---

[3] To use the more precise terminology of Bl. John Henry Cardinal Newman in *A Grammar of Assent*: notional apprehension of an idea is abstract, intellectual, and generalized, while real apprehension of an idea is vivid, specific, and concrete. Real apprehension, or what we can call a grasp of meaning, is the basis for real assent (e.g., belief that God exists), whereas notional apprehension can only support inferences, not belief (e.g., *if* morality really is objective, *then* it is reasonable to conclude that God exists as the source of that morality). We necessarily, and naturally, have only a notional apprehension of many concepts, but this can become real apprehension either through imaginative means or through experience. Much apologetics work is fruitless because the skeptic has only notional apprehension (if that) of the claim that the Christian puts forward. Even worse is the situation in which the Christian, through deficiencies in his or her devotional life, also has only a notional rather than a real apprehension of the very truths for which he argues. This is an occupational hazard of apologetics, and is a reason why apologists must always seek to grow in knowledge and love of God and neighbor—not just in knowledge about God. See Bl. John Henry Cardinal Newman, *An Essay in Aid of a Grammar of Assent* (Worcester, MA: Assumption Press, 2013); first published 1870.

Resurrection may fail to gain traction with a skeptic when the language in play is felt to be so airy and theoretical.

This is where Ward's claim is so critically important: that "apologetic arguments . . . must all be imaginatively realized before they can begin to make traction on the reader's reason, let alone on the reader's will."[4] To most people raised in a secular culture and educated in a secular school system, the words we use to talk about even the most basic principles of the Faith are jargon-words. They have no substantial content for the non-Christian—and indeed, often not much meaning for the Christian either, which is why one of the most important tasks for apologists is catechesis and formation inside the Church. As a result, when apologists have conversations with skeptics about issues of faith, or even when catechists and pastors talk to people in church, there's often a huge, but hidden, meaning gap.

THE MEANING GAP

Here it is worth exploring one apologetics issue in a bit more detail, to show just how wide can be the gap between the meaning we have for a word and the meaning that a skeptic has for it, even for seemingly very ordinary words. Consider: What does it mean to have *faith in God*?

We can define faith as "the assurance of things hoped for, the conviction of things not seen,"[5] but for most skeptics, this definition merely illustrates the problem. If faith is "the assurance of things hoped for," is that not

4 Ward, "The Good Serves the Better and Both the Best."
5 Hebrews 11:1.

an outright admission of Christianity as wish-fulfillment? ("Gotcha!" says the atheist.) Furthermore, "the conviction of things not seen" suggests *blind* faith, because in our culture today—deeply materialistic and naturalistic as it is—'unseen' is for all practical purposes a synonym for 'unreal.' In this view, if something is unseen it cannot be measured, and if it cannot be measured, it doesn't really exist; thus, "the conviction of things unseen" could apply to the existence of fairies and leprechauns just as much as to the existence of God. ("Proof positive that faith is irrational!" says the skeptic.) And so the very definition of faith from Scripture itself seems, to the skeptic, to be a frank admission that faith is unreal: that we are making it all up. It's an empty term, not even worth discussing. ("You poor self-deluded thing," says the atheist.)

Nor is 'God' a more straightforward term. Even if the atheist can get past difficulties with the idea of 'faith,' his concept of 'God' may well be 'cosmic sky-daddy': the idea of an old man in the sky, meting out rewards and punishments. This is (rightly) unbelievable; given *this* idea of 'God,' it is entirely reasonable to assume that 'faith in God' is a cultural construct, a story used to threaten or bribe people into submission, or something that uneducated people believed in before there was Science. Or, for someone who is 'spiritual but not religious,' the word 'God' might be an abstract term for universal goodness. For that person, talking about what God has done in history or how he offers mercy is a non sequitur, along the lines of suggesting that the number three has a wonderful plan for your life.

So we can see that language about 'faith in God' is,

in many cases, as meaningless to the skeptic as talking about 'confidence in snarks and boojums.' At best, the skeptic attempts to be polite about it, the way one might be polite about an adult who seriously claims a belief in leprechauns in the garden, or alleges to have met Shakespeare's Prince Hamlet. There's absolutely no question of genuinely investigating claims of tiny footprints or asking to be invited to dinner with the Dane. The discussion between the atheist and the apologist becomes nothing more than rhetorical maneuvering to trap one or the other into admission of irrationality.

Consider this: if I play a game of Monopoly with a friend, and I land on 'Go to Jail,' I don't have to actually go to jail. If we are playing a war-themed video game and I get shot, nobody has to take me to the emergency room. The games use words that point to real-life experiences, but without the substance of them; the players try to win, and may indeed get very emotional in the process, but fundamentally they know it's a game. If 'God' and 'faith' and all the other concepts that we want to talk about with skeptics are just words to them, such that our argument is just an intellectual game—well, then we will get exactly nowhere, and we will waste a lot of time talking past each other.

The dangers of using religious language without attention to meaning for the listener are not limited to interactions with skeptics; a disjunction of meaning can (and often does) occur in preaching and catechesis within the Church as well. For instance, a young person raised in the Church may have a fuzzy idea of sin as meaning 'hurting other people,' rather than as something objectively wrong in itself that harms one's relationship with

God and injures one's soul. This young person is thus no hypocrite in agreeing with his parents that sin is wrong, while sleeping with his girlfriend. After all, they're consenting adults, so nobody is getting hurt . . . and if nobody is getting hurt, there's no sin! Against this backdrop, arguments about the immorality of his behavior are likely to be met with incomprehension, or result in a conviction that the Church's teachings are arbitrary and can safely be ignored. The disagreement about meaning can hide beneath the surface, distorting the conversation without the participants realizing it.

Pastors, ministry leaders, and teachers may simply assume that terms such as 'faith,' 'salvation,' 'sin,' 'prayer,' and 'resurrection' have shared, real meaning for all those who have professed faith in Christ, when in fact this may not be the case. A persistent failure to attend to meaning within the Church is a real danger to believers on a number of counts. It can lead to a pervasive sense of hypocrisy, if Christians begin to wonder whether anyone really means the words used in worship services or in the creeds; to destructive doubts, if Christians conclude that these words do not have real meaning; or to movement away from orthodoxy and toward various heresies, as a persistent absence of meaning for words like 'resurrection' can lead to a distancing from or even rejection of the historical particularity of Christianity.

What can we do about it?

CREATING MEANING

We must help people find the *words* we use to be meaningful—for the words to be something other than tokens in a game. Then, and only then, will we have a hope of real communication. As Ward explains, "Things must rise up out of the swamp of nonsense into the realm of meaning if the imagination is to get any handle on them. Only then can we begin to judge whether their meanings are true or false. Before anything can be either true or false it must mean."[6] Thus, only when something has meaning, which is generated by the imagination, can we begin to use our reason to judge whether it is true, or false. If someone can find the idea of the supernatural to be meaningful—an idea that can be grasped, that is worth grasping—then, and only then, is the question '*Is it true?*' significant.

But before we explore how to *create* meaning, we should first ask what we mean by the word! In popular usage, it can range from translation (the word gato *means* cat in Spanish) to interpretation (the statement "I don't care for mushrooms" *means* that I find them disgusting) to significance (my dream about being chased by zombies *means* that I'm nervous about my conference presentation). We need a more precise definition of 'meaning.'[7]

For the purposes of apologetics, as for the purposes of writing, it is not the words themselves, but the reader's

---

[6] Ward, "The Good Serves the Better and Both the Best," 61–62.

[7] Some postmodern thinkers seem to suggest that language is so unstable that no claim to a definite meaning is possible at all. We will take no heed of this extreme view, for the eminently practical reason that if the deconstructionists are correct, we have no grounds for interpreting their writings to mean what they seem to mean. However, as even Derrida appears to have something that he intends genuinely to communicate, it seems more reasonable to assume that some degree of meaning can, indeed, be found in the text or through the reader's engagement with the text.

or listener's encounter (or potential encounter) with the words that matters. Some of our conversations on apologetics issues take place 'live,' in personal conversations and public speaking, where we have the opportunity to interact with our listener. Today, however, much apologetics work (perhaps even most) is time-deferred. We write, or record a video clip or an audio lecture, or do an interview, and send our words out into the wider world, to be read or listened to by unknown people at unknown points in the future. Nonetheless, the generation of meaning in all these contexts is relational, even if we never meet the person who reads or hears our words.

Meaningful utterances always have an intended or at least potential audience that is capable of understanding the content presented in the basic sense that it was intended (consciously or unconsciously[8]) by the speaker. 'Meaning,' referring to the degree, or nature, of an individual's grasp of a concept, is both subjective in the sense of being personally experienced, and also objective in the sense that it is still related to the text and to the intended meaning. If I were to read a passage from *Hamlet* aloud to a cat, the words would have no meaning to him in this sense. Certainly, the cat might conclude that my speaking to him is an indication that I've noticed his presence and might feed him if he produces sufficiently plaintive noises; nonetheless, the line "To be or not to be, that is the question" does not *mean* "The human will soon open a can of cat food."

---

[8] It is possible for an author to create works that have meaning beyond what was consciously intended.

A significant part of the apologist's work involves discerning what preconceptions, difficulties, and context the audience is likely to have, so as to write or speak in such a way as to increase the likelihood that the ideas are understood as intended. What grasp does my audience have of the ideas I am presenting? Is my task at this moment to clarify the rational meaning of the ideas, in the sense of propositions and definitions, so as to remove obstacles of basic interpretation? Or is my task to bring the ideas to life, to help people imaginatively grasp them and appreciate their significance? We need not try to do everything at once, but it helps to have an idea of what stage of meaning-making we are engaged in.[9]

The work of creating meaning, then, can be understood broadly as a spectrum of engagement, operating in different ways for different purposes; it is as valuable inside the Church as outside. A more meaningful grasp of essential Christian concepts like forgiveness, peace, love, patience, chastity, hospitality, and so on can enable people to recognize them as vivid and beautiful truths, not just abstract theological points. Imaginative engagement with biblical and doctrinal language can thus help to lead

---

[9] One of the most important questions that an apologist can ask is "What do you mean by that?" (Repeatedly, if necessary!) It is also helpful to listen to how people use words; this can provide hints about the meaning given to them. In particular, we can attend to whether the person seems to be merely using a phrase by rote (whether it is an atheist talking point or a Christian expression), or is using it in ways that show a genuine understanding of the concept. This last point is especially helpful when interacting with Christian students, who are often eager to give the 'right answer' whether or not they know what it means. Often, the work of the apologist and the catechist involves at least as much listening as speaking.

people into personal experience of the reality these words represent, and to grow spiritually as well as intellectually.

An imaginative understanding of bereavement and suffering can also lead to greater sympathy, enabling us more fully to "weep with those who weep."[10] In this way, a person who has never suffered a serious loss may be able to offer genuine comfort to those who are grieving, and someone in good health can recognize how to provide useful support to those enduring chronic illness.

Not to be overlooked is the value of imaginative understanding of sin, so that people can *avoid* gaining personal experience thereof. Indeed, part of the work of ministry is to help people gain meaning for certain truths in the hopes that they will never experience these things for themselves. The imaginative realization of the ugliness of sin can encourage a young person to resist temptations to sexual license or selfishness.

The greatest challenge that apologists face in meaning-making is to make connections for those who know little or nothing of the Faith. Apologists are often faced with a communication challenge because we often work on the borderlands where those we hope to reach do not yet have much, or any, lived experience of the truth being presented. We often have very little to work with. The most straightforward way of presenting truth under these circumstances is propositional and doctrinal, but unfortunately, this is also the way that is most difficult for people to grasp unaided if they lack experience of the reality to which the doctrine points. In order to begin to under-

---

[10] Romans 12:15.

stand a totally new propositional claim, the listener needs to have at least some building-blocks of meaning. The apologist must be willing to start small, and be able to cultivate meaning at different levels and in different ways. In this work, rational and imaginative apologetics are intertwined, as we present the truth in both abstract and imaginatively realized ways. With both the imagination and the intellect engaged, the will has a solid foundation upon which to act.

Can this creation of meaning be done? Yes. Let me offer a deliberately trivial example.

Consider the word 'tea.' For me, as an American, until a few years ago, I'd never had a proper cup of tea. If I'd relied on my own experiences, I would have quite concluded that it's a far inferior beverage to coffee, and not worth bothering about. From my experiences, this was a rational conclusion: a Lipton's tea bag in a styrofoam cup with lukewarm water creates a beverage of sorts, but not one to be enthusiastic about.

However, as someone who loves British literature and culture, I frequently encountered the idea of 'tea' in literary contexts that made it seem more appealing. By the time I finally visited England for myself, the word 'tea' had acquired sufficient meaning—thanks to authors like Jane Austen and Anthony Trollope—that I eagerly desired to have a proper cup. Rather than not bothering with it, I sought it out . . . and discovered proper British tea is something totally different than what I'd encountered before. Good, plain English breakfast tea, made with *boiling* water, and with milk (not cream), results in something entirely different from the sad American version. And the British make sure that wherever you go, you can make a proper cup of tea: every hotel room, bed and breakfast, and even college lodgings have an electric tea-kettle, a mug, and a supply of tea. It took a little while for me to fully appreciate it, but I could tell right away that it was worth making the effort. In the end, I came to enjoy tea so much that I now drink it every day, and even without sugar.

My imaginative engagement with the idea of tea made me aware that the word might *mean* something more interesting than I thought, and my subsequent investigation changed the way I live my life (albeit in a very small way). What happened for 'tea' is, in a trivial way, the same sort of thing that happened for me with infinitely more important words like 'prayer,' 'grace,' and 'Eucharist,' both in my conversion from atheism to Christian faith and in my growth as a Christian.

PINNING DOWN MEANING

How, then, do we encourage this sort of shift to happen? We can start by considering how we understand words at all. Language is always understood contextually; the development of meaning involves the reader's prior knowledge and experience; and a word always has multiple potential meanings.

For example, to continue our beverage theme, the word 'coffee,' a perfectly ordinary noun, is a word for which we might expect the reader to have a single, uncontested meaning. Certainly it does not invite the range of interpretation that a word like 'faith' does. Even so, 'coffee' does not have a one-to-one correspondence with a precise, unchanging item in the physical world. For one person, it might be a mug of brewed coffee; for another, coffee from a French press; for another, a tiny cup of espresso. It might even be that terrible impostor called instant coffee. The range is significant, but it is seldom a problem (except perhaps for jet-lagged travelers). The cultural context sets up expectations for the actual coffee-drinker; the literary context both sets up expectations and allows for flexibility of interpretation for the reader. If I'm reading an eighteenth century novel that has a scene in a coffee-shop (or 'coffee house' as they used to call them then), it's not necessary for me to know exactly what means of preparation the author had in mind; my own experiences with the beverage will allow me to imagine the scene with reasonable, if not total, accuracy.

Other words have a much wider range of possible meanings. Notably, the words that we use to talk about the Faith are nearly always rich, dark, and creamy with many layers of meaning, both explicit and implicit. Thus, far more than with words like 'tea' or 'coffee,' words about theology, faith, doctrine, worship, and devotion have the potential to be misunderstood, because of inadequate or missing context, or as a result of certain assumptions or experiences on the part of the reader or listener. However, we need not, on this ground, try to avoid the richness and multiplicity of meaning that language offers us. Indeed, we must not, because if we do, we will destroy our nascent meaning-making before it has a chance to do any good. Consider, for instance, what is perhaps the greatest single sentence ever written: "And the Word became flesh, and dwelt among us, and we have seen his glory, the glory as of a father's only son, full of grace and truth."[11] Each word of this overwhelmingly important statement from St. John's Gospel is resonant and evocative, and demonstrates the power of multiple overlapping meanings. Re-phrased into technical theological language, this pre-eminently meaningful sentence would be useful in certain specific contexts, but would become much more limited, and less engaging, in the process. We can say that the Second Person of the Trinity became incarnate, and this is true, but it is a flat statement compared to these words of St. John.

More importantly, though, total precision in language is impossible. Language is not mathematics, and attempts to force language into a kind of mathematical precision will always fail. To use 'H_2O' instead of the word 'water' is more precise but less richly meaningful; it reflects only one aspect of the word, that of water as understood from a scientific perspective. This is an important perspective, to be sure: the chemist or geologist discussing the action of water in relation to other substances needs to be able to refer to its molecular composition. Poetic language would, in those circumstances, be a hindrance. But 'H_2O' is just one way of looking at water, not the only one. As soon as we consider water in other contexts, more meaning comes flooding in: water as quencher of thirst, water for washing in, water in the garden-hose, in Baptism, in the swimming-pool, water for drowning in, for cataclysms like tsunamis, and so on and so forth. Words never mean just one thing and one thing only, but carry with them ideas, associations, and connections that provide the raw material

---

[11] John 1:14.

that a gifted poet can use to convey more meaning than the word, by itself, can hold.

In the right context, multiple *correct* meanings can operate simultaneously; it is a characteristic not just of literature but of language itself that words do not have precise semantic boundaries. The greatest authors are able to use these multiple meanings to resonate with each other. Consider Shakespeare's Sonnet 73, a moving reflection on age and youth, which opens with a striking image:

> That time of year thou mayst in me behold
> When yellow leaves, or none, or few, do hang
> Upon those boughs which shake against the cold,
> Bare ruined choirs, where late the sweet birds sang.

The last line means *literally* a ruined building which, before winter's coming, had *literal* birds perched on it. But it is more than that: as the "ruined choirs" were those of the abbeys destroyed by Henry VIII in the dissolution of the monasteries, the line also refers to a *literal* ruin (the abbey) with *figurative* birds: that is, the monks or nuns who would have sung the Divine Office there. It is furthermore a *figurative* ruin with *figurative* birds: an image of an old man whose limbs no longer sing with beauty, now that it is the winter of his life. All three levels work together, creating a richly textured image that is melancholy with a strong undercurrent of bitterness and loss.

In the richness of language, we find not a problem, but an opportunity for creating meaning, because God has so made us that we can continue to create imaginative literature to body forth meaning in words. And even as we create imaginative literature, and respond to it, we are giving glory to God who made us in his image. God is the Creator, the ultimate Author and Artist. As J. R. R. Tolkien put it, we are "sub-creators": "we make in our measure and in our derivative mode, because we are made: and not only made, but made in the image and likeness of a Maker."[12]

EVENSONG IN OXFORD ON ST. CECILIA'S DAY

"My soul doth magnify the Lord," we sing,
And offer back, in music's common voice,
The melody He made; the gift we bring
Is wholly His—and so we dare rejoice
With Mary's words, entrusting her with all
Our hopes and fears, to prism them to praise
Before her Son, her Lord and ours. We call
On her, with nothing of our own, to pray;
And then, still prisoned in our lonely selves,
We hear the piercing note of joy that calls
Us home, with all the saints, to live, and dwell . . .
And so we sing, and let the silence fall,
To be redeemed. On these our broken words,
Miserable and weak, have mercy, Lord.

---

[12] Tolkien, "On Fairy-stories," 66.

CHAPTER THREE

LANGUAGE AND METAPHOR

IMAGINATIVE literature is a particularly valuable means of creating meaning for ideas, as well as for conveying these ideas to people who would be resistant to them if presented as arguments. C. S. Lewis's Chronicles of Narnia are a stellar example of this approach. As Lewis put it in "Sometimes Fairy Stories May Say Best What's to Be Said":

> I thought I saw how stories of this kind [fairy tales] could steal past a certain inhibition which had paralysed much of my own religion in childhood. Why did one find it so hard to feel as one was told one ought to feel about God or about the sufferings of Christ? I thought the chief reason was that one was told one ought to. An obligation to feel can freeze feelings. And reverence itself did harm. The whole subject was associated with lowered voices; almost as if it were something medical. But supposing that by casting all these things into an imaginary world, stripping them of their stained-glass and Sunday school associations, one

could make them for the first time appear in their real potency? Could one not thus steal past the watchful dragons? I thought one could.[1]

Now, Lewis himself is quite clear that his approach is not a simplistic one, describing as "pure moonshine" the idea that he "drew up a list of basic Christian truths and hammered out 'allegories' to embody them."[2] How, then, did he manage to make the Chronicles so deeply meaningful, conveying so vividly and attractively ideas such as the Incarnation, the creation of the world, and the ideas of resurrection, repentance, and salvation?

He did not simply dress up Christian ideas, or (worse) have characters preach to one another, but rather he created stories that *embodied* Christian ideas—in particular, the character of Christ, through the imagery of the seven medieval planets, as Michael Ward has demonstrated.[3] The kingly nature of Christ, associated with Jupiter, is expressed in *The Lion, the Witch and the Wardrobe*; the illuminating wisdom of Christ, associated with the Sun, is expressed in *The Voyage of the 'Dawn Treader'*; and the children in each story, as they learn to love the Christ-like Aslan, gradually take on his Christ-like qualities, becoming kings and queens in *Lion*, drinking light in *Voyage*, and so on and so forth. The effect of Lewis's subtle but

---

[1] C. S. Lewis, "Sometimes Fairy Stories May Say Best What's to Be Said," in *On Stories and Other Essays on Literature*, ed. Walter Hooper (Orlando, FL: Harcourt, 1966), 47.

[2] Ibid., 46.

[3] Michael Ward, *Planet Narnia: The Seven Heavens in the Imagination of C. S. Lewis* (Oxford: Oxford University Press, 2008).

persistent Christological focus is that the reader, probably without consciously realizing it, gains a sense of the meaning of who Christ is, what the Incarnation is, and what grace is in the life of the believer. Certainly that was the case for me.[4]

Here we return to the question again: how did Lewis do it? How, indeed, do any writers of imaginative literature breathe meaning into the words and ideas that they present to the reader? One of the ways that Lewis accomplishes his aims is by making use of symbolism, metaphor, and imagery, woven into his stories. It behooves us to take a moment to consider how these literary devices work—especially since figurative language is one of the primary modes by which, past and present, the Church uses to communicate truth to her people, in Scripture, Christian art, and the liturgy.

CONFUSION AND CLARIFICATION

Similes, metaphors, images, and so on are literary devices; they are examples of figurative language. Before we go even a step further, we must stop and attend very carefully to precisely what 'figurative' means, because there's a great deal of confusion among Christians about the way that literal and figurative language works.

Most Christians have encountered, at some point, the sarcastic cry of "You can't possibly take that *literally*, can you?" It's an all-purpose rejection, used for anything in Scripture or Church teaching that the person can't accept. "So," the skeptic says, "your Bible says that on the seventh

[4] See my memoir, *Not God's Type: An Atheist Academic Lays Down Her Arms* (San Francisco: Ignatius Press, 2014).

day of creation, God rested. Does that mean he was tired? How can I believe in some old guy up in the sky?" "Not really," the Christian replies, "God didn't actually get tired, but . . ." "Aha! So then you don't *literally* believe what the Bible says, do you? I knew it! You Christians are all hypocrites." "No, wait. . . ." And on the flip side, "That's just a metaphor!" is another way to avoid coming to terms with the Church's teaching on something from Scripture, such as the Real Presence of Christ in the Eucharist.[5] The resulting dialogue may well degenerate into "It's a metaphor! No, it's not!"—going exactly nowhere. The problem is that these retorts are based on a misunderstanding of what a metaphor actually *is*, and indeed what the word 'literally' means.

To begin with the word 'literally,' we must consider both what the word itself means, and also the difference between literal and figurative language.

In literary terms, the 'literal' meaning is *the meaning which the author intends.* We will call this meaning of 'literal' Sense 1.[6] The author may intend his words to be interpreted either factually or imaginatively; the trick is to understand the intention. Most people, most of the time, are able to do this naturally and immediately, without overthinking it; we take it for granted, and rightly so. What makes it funny that Don Quixote tilts at windmills, thinking they are giants, is that he is taking old chivalric romances as *fact* when we, the readers, know they should be read as *fiction.*

Understanding what the author intends is, essential-

---

5 John 6:35–58; Matthew 26:26–28; Mark 14:22–24; Luke 22:19–20; 1 Corinthians 11:23–30.

6 See C. S. Lewis, *Studies in Words* (Cambridge: Cambridge University Press, 1960). I have adopted his approach.

ly, a question of identifying and understanding the genre. Satire, fantasy, and poetry are genres that are to some degree 'non-realistic' (without getting into a debate about what 'realistic' means). Identifying genre is not difficult if one has sufficient awareness of context. The Psalms are poetry; Kenneth Grahame's *The Wind in the Willows* is a fantasy; Jonathan Swift's "A Modest Proposal" is a satire. For any reader who is minimally aware of the conventions of literature, and paying minimal attention, it is self-evident that the Psalmist, in describing God as a "rock," is not advocating the worship of boulders; that an exploration of the English countryside will not (alas) turn up small mammals dressed in Edwardian clothes having picnics; and that Swift was not advocating eating Irish babies as a means of solving a population crisis. The fact that some people (such as college undergraduates) might at least for a moment think that Swift was serious doesn't change the fact that he intended his work to be read as satire. The *literal* (Sense 1) reading of these works requires a recognition that they express their points using *figurative* techniques.

We may, at times, wish to argue for a *non-literal* interpretation of a text as an additional layer of meaning on top of what the author intends or what the genre suggests. Such readings can be both legitimate and meaningful, if they can be supported from the evidence of the text, are coherent, and do not contradict or undermine the literal (Sense 1) meaning of the text. The tradition of the Church, for instance, holds that the Song of Songs can be understood in terms of the love of Christ for his Church, which is a meaning that the human author could not (chronologically) have intended, but that is beautifully consistent with the poem as a whole. Even for non-sacred writings, it is possible for a writer to put more into a story or poem than he or she is consciously aware.

Thus, this is Sense 1 of 'literal': understood in reference to the author's meaning and the genre and form in which the work is written.

The somewhat confusing second meaning of literal, which we will call Sense 2, is *expressing an idea directly without an intermediate step of interpretation.* In this sense, it contrasts with figurative language, which expresses an idea indirectly and requires an additional act of interpretation.

It's the difference between expressing poverty with "I have only ten dollars in my checking account" (literal, direct) and "I'm as poor as a church mouse" (figurative, indirect); hunger with "I'm very hungry" (literal) and "I could eat a horse" (figurative); or admiration with "She is young and beautiful" (literal) and "My love is like a red, red rose / that's newly sprung in June" (figurative). You get the picture. And in 'getting the picture' you have understood my meaning *literally* (Sense 1) because you recognized that 'acquiring a drawing or other visual depiction of my point' was a figurative expression for understanding it.

An illustration of the two meanings of 'literal' is somewhat amusingly provided by one of the quirks of recent slang usage: the expansion of the meaning of 'literally' in common usage to become a simple intensifier, as in the sentence: "It was so hot today that I literally melted!" We can see a useful illustration of my point here. If we take the word 'literally' in this sentence as Sense 2, then it's absurd: the speaker did not, in fact, melt into a pile of goo. The pedant would say, "Well, no—you *figuratively* melted!" But the fact that the speaker used *literally* in this way doesn't mean he's an idiot who doesn't understand the difference between literal and figurative language. Rather, he's aware that his audience will understand *literally* as meaning something along the lines of 'felt like' or 'came close to'—and that's in fact the case. None of his friends will blanch with horror and say, "You actually melted? Are you okay? Do you need to go to the hospital for a checkup?" In short, the speaker was trusting his hearers to interpret his words with Sense 1: that is, with an awareness of the meaning the speaker intended: that it's an unpleasantly hot day.

There is no such thing as completely literal (Sense 2) language; figurative elements are an intrinsic, inseparable part of every aspect of our speech. Consider, for instance, that in understanding the point that I'm making, you intuitively recognize that by 'point' I do not mean a sharply tapered object, but rather a figurative expression of the key insight. All use of language beyond the most basic functional utterances involves some use of figurative speech, at some level. So far, so good. However, there is no such thing as completely figurative language, either, because some aspect of any figure of speech has to be traced back to the literal sense, in order to provide the necessary connection between image and idea. For instance, when I referred to a 'key insight,' it was a figurative expression, but the meaning comes via analogy to the literal object: just as a physical key opens a closed door and allows us to go through, so too a 'key' insight 'opens' a subject so that we can understand it more deeply. I am not a linguist nor a philologist, so I will not venture even to speculate on how all this works, or how the different parts of language relate to each other; I do know, as a literary critic and a writer, that it *is* so.

The distinction between literal (Sense 2) and figurative language is not one of better/worse, true/untrue, or accurate/less accurate; rather, it is a distinction between ways that the author or speaker chooses to convey his idea. It is, in fact, very much the same distinction as between philosophical and imaginative approaches to apologetics. Both literal and figurative modes are necessary and important, because they convey different aspects of the truth, and are complementary to each other.

Figurative language is a mode of conveying an idea, not an avoidance of it. When Jesus says, "I am the Way" or "I am the true vine,"[7] he uses an image that brings to mind a road or grapevine, because that conveys an important insight about who he is and how we relate to him. Jesus is not suggesting that he is *actually* a paved path through the wilderness or a fruiting bush. Such an interpretation is recognizably in error because it makes his statement nonsensical or trivial. Rather, the statement is metaphorical, and it is *in* the metaphor that the truth is being conveyed, and so it's not possible to dodge the claims of Jesus by saying they are 'just' metaphorical.

Here it is important to note that while figurative language is a vehicle to convey meaning, the underlying reality is reflected by, not created by, the use of language. Owen Barfield writes in *Poetic Diction* that there is such a thing as a 'true metaphor':

[7] John 14:6; 15:1.

> Men do not *invent* those mysterious relations be-
> tween separate external objects, and between ob-
> jects and feelings or ideas, which it is the function
> of poetry to reveal. These relations exist inde-
> pendently, not indeed of Thought, but of any in-
> dividual thinker.[8]

As imaginative apologists, our task is to make use of true metaphors, whether we create them ourselves, or discover them in the work of poets, novelists, and screenwriters.

The beauty of figurative language, used well, is that it can communicate truth both directly and intuitively, by its fittingness of image and meaning, even if the reader doesn't consciously understand it. There are many different literary devices that fall under the descriptive category of 'figurative language': metaphor, simile, images, symbols, personification, and allegory, for instance. We will now focus on simile and metaphor, as these will best repay our attention. Most of the other types of figurative language that I've mentioned can be understood as variants of metaphor.

A metaphor is a comparison (by means of a statement of identity) of one thing to a second thing that is outwardly *dissimilar* to the first but that has some inner likeness to it, in order to convey something true about the first thing. For instance, consider "The Lord is my shepherd"[9] or "Your word is a lamp to my feet and a light to my path." A simile is nearly the same, but uses the words

---

[8] Barfield, *Poetic Diction*, 86.
[9] Psalm 23:1.

'like' or 'as,' which make the comparison explicit, as in the words that God spoke to the prophet Jeremiah: "As the clay is in the potter's hand, so you are in mine, House of Israel."[10] Similes and metaphors are potent because they can hold a great deal of meaning packed into a very small space.

LOOKING IN DETAIL

Let's take a look at a single image, that of a lion, which is used by scriptural authors both in similes and metaphors. The lion appears frequently in Scripture; for instance, we have "Like a roaring lion your adversary the devil prowls around, looking for someone to devour";[11] "Rescue me from their ravages, my life from the lions!";[12] "The wicked flee when no one pursues, but the righteous are as bold as a lion";[13] Jesus is "the Lion of the tribe of Judah."[14]

In order to appreciate how metaphor works, it's helpful to approach it circuitously. Let's put our lion through its paces.

Fairly obviously, "A lion is a large cat" or "A lion is a meat-eater" are not metaphors, but rather literal (Sense 2) statements: definitions or descriptions. Likewise, "A lion is a tiger" is not a metaphor, but another literal statement, although in this case apparently false, since the two words understood literally mean two different kinds of animals. (I say 'apparently' false, because such a seemingly

[10] Jeremiah 18:6.
[11] 1 Peter 5:8.
[12] Psalm 35:17.
[13] Proverbs 28:1.
[14] Revelation 5:5.

false statement could be the opening to an argument that we have misunderstood what lions are all along—perhaps, according to the zoologist, they really are tigers, just ones who have lost their stripes. But the point is that a good writer would know that his reader would have this reaction, and would explain or qualify the statement: "A lion is *technically* a tiger, because. . . .")

"A lion is a *león*" is not a metaphor, or indeed figurative language of any kind, but rather an identification of the word in a different language (Spanish). In both cases, the word refers to the large African cat; there is no difference in meaning between the two. (This is worth noting in life-issues discussions; to the claim that "it's not a baby, it's just a fetus," one possible response is to point out that 'fetus' is simply the Latin word for 'baby.')

"A lion is *like* a tiger" is neither a metaphor nor a simile, because it is comparing two similar, not dissimilar, things. It's a literal statement, one that could be used either to explain a lion to someone who has not seen one ("It is like a tiger, but without stripes") or to begin a discussion of the distinctive features of each, such as the presence or absence of a mane, or living in prides. "A lion is a fruitcake" is also not a metaphor, but rather nonsense, since the comparison is between two entirely dissimilar things; the comparison does not shed light on either term.

Finally, we come to clearly figurative language: "The devil is like a roaring lion" is a vivid simile, in this case helping us to recognize that Satan is dangerous and predatory. "The lion is the king of beasts" is a metaphor, like our Scriptural examples. It does not mean that the lion wears a small crown and receives fealty from the other animals; it means that the lion is a noble, powerful beast that displays characteristics that we associate with human royalty. Before the scientific revolution, writers and people in general were much more inclined than nowadays to anthropomorphize animals: to see the lion as kingly, the fox as sly, the peacock as proud, and so on. We can see this in the medieval bestiaries and in stories like Aesop's fables. It is worth emphasizing that this pre-modern anthropomorphizing was not the result of people in those days being ignorant about animals. In fact, people in medieval times and earlier were much more likely to have first-hand observations of wildlife (not to mention domestic animals) than the modern city- or suburb-dweller. Metaphors convey interpretations and significance, not bare facts. "The lion is the king of the beasts" tells something true (and meaningful) both about our perception of the lion and about the lion's place in its ecosystem.

Lastly, Aslan the lion in the Chronicles of Narnia is neither a symbol nor a metaphor for Christ; Lewis has constructed the stories so that Aslan *is* Christ in the world of Narnia. Lewis has not chosen at random, however; Aslan's lion-ness evokes certain associations and impressions that he wants his reader to have for Christ. As we can see, these different literary techniques can overlap and blur into each other; this is art, not mathematics.[15]

---

[15] Another non-metaphor: "Aslan is on the move. You won't find him lion around doing nothing." Puns are either the highest, or the lowest, form of wordplay; take your pick.

USING METAPHOR

I've walked you through all these different iterations of lions so that you can see more clearly the way that figurative language *works*. I'm going to focus now on *metaphor*, because it is the one that gets most attention in apologetics, and because it is the most broadly applicable for apologetics. The insights we gain about metaphor can be applied to other types of figurative language, from symbols and images to personification and allegory. By having a basic understanding of how metaphor works, we will better understand how it is that imaginative approaches can convey truth—and can do so in such effective ways.

Dissimilarity-with-inner-likeness is the key feature of metaphor, the feature that is constructive of meaning. Notice that in all cases, it's necessary to have basic knowledge of the second item, and for a metaphor to work most effectively, it's necessary to have knowledge of both items. If I were to say, "A lion is a felisaurinoid," you might not be able to tell immediately whether this is a literal statement, a metaphor, or nonsense. Of course, 'felisaurinoid' is a word I made up, but since it begins with the Latin for 'cat,' you might have had an instant of being unsure about what sort of statement this was. Until you've come to a conclusion about the meaning (or lack thereof) of 'felisaurinoid,' you can't assess the statement.

The metaphor "he is a lion in battle" finds an inner likeness in two dissimilar things, a man and an animal. What does the sentence mean? If we were to translate the metaphor into more literal language, we would say, "he is ferocious and dangerous, but also awe-inspiring, beautiful, and noble." (Contrast "he is a lion in battle" with "he is a hyena in battle.") Metaphorical language conveys meaning through this transference, and normally the metaphor is so instantly comprehensible that we don't need to go through the process of actual translation. If we do not know Christ, but have seen a lion at a zoo or at least seen television documentaries of lions, the phrase "the Lion of Judah" can convey meaning that the phrase "the Lord God" does not. (It helps if we know what 'Judah' refers to, of course! However, even an imperfect grasp of the metaphor allows for some useful associations to come through.)

Metaphor is a literary device, just like rhyme is a literary device; as such, it is a means of expressing ideas that may be true or false, effective or ineffective, compelling or boring. The use of metaphor (like the use of rhyme, allegory, narrative, and so on) does not in itself have anything to do with whether the idea being conveyed is true or false. We still have to assess the meaning of the metaphorical statement, just as we have to assess the meaning of a propositional statement. We must ask, "Is it true?" in each case; recognizing what kind of statement it is will help us to judge rightly.

Metaphors are valuable because they build a bridge between the known and the unknown. Or, to put it another way, metaphors serve the same purpose as propositional statements: to orient the reader toward reality. C. S. Lewis makes the point that Christian theology itself is not as directly powerful or exciting as a personal spiritual experience, but it is necessary all the same: "Doctrines are not God: they are only a kind of map . . . [but] if you want to get any further, you must use the map."[16] It may be more pleasant to dwell on spiritual feelings without thinking about doctrine, but, Lewis continues, "you will not get eternal life by simply feeling the presence of God in flowers and music. Neither will you get anywhere by looking at maps without going to sea. Nor will you be very safe if you go to sea without a map."[17]

A metaphor is like a map, as well: one that is drawn in a different style than a doctrinal statement, but a map nonetheless, intended to help the reader arrive at the truth. A beautifully drawn and illustrated map will attract the eye, but not as an end in itself; rather, the map helps readers to discover where they are—perhaps to realize that, in fact, they have gotten lost!—and it helps them get where they want, or need, to go.

METAPHORS AND CONTEXT

Because metaphors and similes work by relating the known to the unknown, using the concrete to convey the meaning of the abstract, it is necessary to know one's audience in order to choose and use them effectively. What works for one time, place, and audience may or may not be helpful for another time, place, or audience. If your audience has a different meaning for one of the elements of a metaphor, then they will not make the right imaginative connection. Images of the ocean and its waves, for instance, might evoke ideas of danger or solitude for

[16] C. S. Lewis, *Mere Christianity*, 1952 (New York: HarperOne, 2001), 154.
[17] Ibid., 155.

readers experienced with sailing (consider the elegiac An-
glo-Saxon poem "The Seafarer"), but suggest relaxation
on holiday for others.

Consider two of Jesus's most famous parables, that of
the Good Samaritan and the Prodigal Son. The Parable
of the Good Samaritan[18] teaches us how we are to treat
our neighbor; Jesus knows full well that his listeners understand the context and how they are to interpret his
teaching. Their knowledge of the genre of the parable
(understanding it literally, Sense 1: as the author intends)
allows them to understand that when Jesus says, "Go and
do likewise," he is giving a broader moral command, beyond directing us to help stranded travelers. It is worth
emphasizing that in the context of the parable, the lawyer
who asks for clarification already knows the truth in propositional form: he is to love his neighbor. What is missing
for this man is a sense of the *meaning* of the command. It
is this meaning that Jesus provides, with the image of the
wounded man and his Samaritan rescuer.

Thus, the effectiveness of the parable for the audience depends on the audience knowing (and accepting)
that in theory they should indeed love their neighbor as
themselves, but being hesitant to accept the full ramifi-
cations of that command: to love those who are different
from them, or those whom it is difficult or inconvenient
to love. The parable was not intended to convince people
that they *should* love their neighbor in the first place, although it may well help to do that.

In modern-day cultural apologetics, this parable may

[18] Luke 10:25–37.

have lost some of its punch, because 'Samaritan' has no resonance for us; it's just the name of the helpful character. In order to be compelling, it may be useful for the apologist to translate the terms of the story, making the characters a conservative Christian and a gay activist, for instance; or a homeless man and a businessman; or a white police officer and a black youth—with either one or the other in the role of Samaritan or wounded man, depending on the audience. Then the parable might have the unsettling effect that it did for its original hearers, making them broaden their idea of 'neighbor' to include those who are different from themselves.

Even so, in some contexts, the audience may not be sufficiently in accord with the basic premise to find the parable helpful. If fear, self-interest, or indifference have taken root in someone's soul, he may not be able to appreciate the meaning of this parable at all . . . and so the apologist must address even deeper issues to start with.

Now consider the Parable of the Prodigal Son,[19] which gives us a powerful extended metaphor about what it means that God is our loving Father. It is a potent way to convey what may otherwise be incomprehensible to most people because they lack real meaning for most of the terms: that God, the Creator of the universe, loves you, and wants you to repent of your sins and relate to him again as a loving Father. (Consider the fact that many people lack any real meaning for the terms 'God,' 'love,' 'repent,' and 'sin.')

But in order for people to most fully grasp the mean-

[19] Luke 15:11–32.

ing of the parable, they need to have an idea of the second term of the metaphor, 'father,' that includes things like 'he provides for me and my mother, he loves me, he protects me,' and so on. Such an understanding helps the reader to make the connection and grasp the extravagant, boundless love and forgiveness of God the Father. But with the breakdown of traditional families in the West, there may be no father in the picture at all for many of the people we want to reach. The Parable of the Prodigal Son will be more difficult to understand by someone for whom 'father' means 'one of my mother's ex-boyfriends.'

We need to find many different ways to talk about God that help people understand his love, his concern, his grace, in ways that they can relate to, all the while keeping our theology orthodox. C. S. Lewis is a brilliant model for this kind of metaphor-making. Michael Ward notes that:

> A brief survey of *Mere Christianity* supplies the following list: becoming a Christian (passing over from life to death) is like joining a campaign of sabotage, like falling at someone's feet or putting yourself in someone's hands, like taking on board fuel or food, like laying down your rebel arms and surrendering, saying sorry, laying yourself open, turning full speed astern; it is like killing part of yourself, like learning to walk or to write, like buying God a present with his own money; it is like a drowning man clutching at a rescuer's hand, like a tin soldier or a statue coming alive, like waking after a long sleep, like getting close to someone or becoming infected, like dressing up or pretending

or playing; it is like emerging from the womb or hatching from an egg; it is like a compass needle swinging to north, or a cottage being made into a palace, or a field being plowed and resown, or a horse turning into a Pegasus, or a greenhouse roof becoming bright in the sunlight; it is like coming around from anesthetic, like coming in out of the wind, like going home.[20]

Is it any wonder that *Mere Christianity* has had such a powerful effect on so many readers? It is not simply that Lewis can explain Christian doctrine clearly and logically—though he certainly does. It is that he provides a superabundance of vivid images and metaphors that engage both the imagination and the reason, so that the ideas he is presenting become richly meaningful. The ideas stick . . . and this gives people the time, opportunity, and motivation to keep thinking about them, to ask more questions, and to discover the truth of these ideas.

Every culture and time needs fresh images and fresh metaphors. Many of Lewis's metaphors still work every bit as well today as they did in the 1940s. But not all of them— nor would he have expected that they would. He was not communicating to a generic audience, but to the very specific audience of men and women in wartime Britain. What images will work best today, in twenty-first-century America and Britain and the rest of the world? That is up to us to find out, and to put them to good use.

---

[20] Michael Ward, "Escape to Wallaby Wood: C. S. Lewis's Depictions of Conversion," 151.

MAPS

Antique maps, with curlicues of ink
As borders, framing what we know, like pages
From a book of travelers' tales: look,
Here in the margin, tiny ships at sail.
No-nonsense maps from family trips: each state
Traced out in color-coded numbered highways,
A web of roads with labeled city-dots
Punctuating the route and its slow stories.
Now GPS puts me right at the center,
A Ptolemaic shift in my perspective.
Pinned where I am, right now, somewhere, I turn
And turn to orient myself. I have
Directions calculated, maps at hand:
Hopelessly lost till I look up at last.

·❖·

CHAPTER FOUR

DISTORTIONS OF MEANING

OUR work as imaginative apologists has both a creative, generative aspect and a defensive, corrective aspect. As we have seen, finding a statement *meaningful* necessarily precedes judgment about the truth or falsity of that statement. However, not only must we do the difficult work of meaning-making in our Christian apologetics, we must also fight against the distortion of language—whether intentional or unintentional—that so often undermines or confuses our message. In fact, we must work hard even to be heard at all.

Materialism has so thoroughly invaded our culture that the fate of one's eternal soul is no longer a pressing issue for most non-believers. A 'spiritual but not religious' person may have a vague sense that all will be well, and so the question is not worth bothering with; the materialist believes that there is no such thing as a soul, and after death, there will be no part of 'you' to be anywhere at all. In either case, the ideas of hell and heaven are not sufficiently in focus to make most non-believers interested in pursuing the question. In contrast, people who couldn't care less about who Christ is often have very strong visceral (and usually negative) reactions to Catholic teaching on ethical and social issues such as the sanctity of human life, marriage, sexuality, contraception, and what it means to be a man or a woman.

Nonetheless, it's not accurate to say that the people who reject Christian moral teachings are amoral or apathetic; in fact, the same people who find the very concept of sin to be incomprehensible or irrelevant often have passionate views about the environment, economic inequalities, social justice, and racism. Since the Church has quite a lot to say on social, economic, and environmental issues as well—because our Faith encompasses all of reality, not just the 'spiritual' bits—it might seem that these issues are an excellent place to engage with non-believers. However, it is an approach that is fraught with difficulties.

It has become difficult for Christians to be heard if they address any moral issues in Christian terms, because the very language used to discuss the subject has become so distorted, even corrupted, that our arguments are brushed aside, ruled out as bigoted and intolerant, or reinterpreted in order to fall in line with the secular version of the argument.

This state of affairs is not, I think, accidental. As Owen Barfield says in *Poetic Diction*, "Of all devices for dragooning the human spirit, the least clumsy is to procure its abortion in the womb of language."[1] It is in the "womb of language" that ideas are conceived, and then can grow and develop. The wider, richer, and more precise our

---

[1] Barfield, *Poetic Diction*, 23.

vocabulary is, the more we will be able to use it to express ideas clearly and reflect on them deeply. Unfortunately, our language is subject to verbicide—the 'murder' of words through exaggeration or mis-use, so that the original meaning is lost.[2] Verbicide can kill words by distortion as well as by watering down their meaning, as in the use of 'sinful' to mean 'enjoyable.' If a delicious slice of chocolate cake can be 'sinfully good,' then the word 'sin' has no real meaning at all.

Verbicide can occur through carelessness, but it can also be deliberately cultivated by those who find it in their interests to render certain words empty of meaning. Authentic debate and discussion—like authentic democracy—are messy and discomfiting processes that require confronting ideas that are disagreeable, and accepting that you can't always have things your own way. To raise an issue for discussion and argument means at least tacitly accepting that you might not be able to convince the other side that you're right . . . and having to live with that. The alternative to authentic discussion is to manipulate circumstances such that the debate never happens, and the position that you favor becomes entrenched—or to manipulate language so that the other point of view becomes unsayable and eventually unthinkable.

Thus, apologists must be prepared to deal not just with arguments and misunderstandings, but also with the conscious or unconscious manipulation and corruption of language.

---

[2] See C. S. Lewis, *An Experiment in Criticism* (Cambridge: Cambridge University Press, 1961).

SLOGANS

One of the ways that language can be manipulated is through the use of slogans. Consider the words used to talk about abortion, such as 'my choice,' 'women's rights,' or 'reproductive freedom.' For end-of-life issues, think of the terms 'assisted suicide' and 'death with dignity.' 'Assisted suicide' is in fact an oxymoron: suicide means self-killing, and if one receives assistance in such a killing, then it's no longer suicide: it's manslaughter or murder. 'Legal murder,' however, is not an attractive phrase. The fact that suicide is, in general, still regarded as a tragedy (at least when it is done by young or talented people) is probably the reason why 'assisted suicide' seems to be fading out as a catchphrase. 'Death with dignity' is a more difficult slogan to counter. Choices, rights, freedom, and dignity are all positive-sounding things, so from the outset, we must struggle with the perception that valuing human life from conception to natural death means being anti-choice, anti-rights, anti-freedom, anti-dignity.

Hidden in these labels is the deep-seated assumption that personal autonomy is the highest good, one that trumps all others. Choices, in this view, are always good in themselves, independent of whether the choice is for good or for bad. Freedom is conceived of as freedom from restraint—without consideration of the purpose of that freedom.

Here, we should consider a question: are *all* catch-phrases and slogans manipulative? After all, the phrase 'pro-life' is supposed to sound positive—who wouldn't be in favor life? It's important to remember that the art of rhetoric is, by itself, neutral: it can be used for good or evil, to make either truth or falsehood memorable. If a phrase or slogan captures the position it represents with reasonable accuracy, it is not manipulative. I was in England during the 2016 referendum about Brexit, and one of the things that I was pleased to see was the fairness of the language used to represent each position. One side was 'Remain' and the other was 'Leave,' with the slogans of 'Stronger Together' and 'Take Back Control,' respectively. The names and slogans were in each case a concise and accurate version of their argument for Britain remaining in or leaving the European Union (whether or not one agreed with the argument).

If we consider the implications of 'pro-life' and 'pro-choice,' though, we can see a difference.

The phrase 'pro-choice' is manipulative because it is not about 'choice' in general, but about the specific choice of abortion. If we examine the term more closely, we see that 'pro-choice' is really just a convenient shorthand for 'being in favor of a woman's freedom to choose to kill her unborn child without legal sanctions.' If it were simply about 'a woman's freedom to choose,' it would be an empty phrase. Pregnant mothers have always had, and will always have, the freedom to choose whether to sustain or terminate the life of their unborn child. Before abortion was decriminalized in 1973, the choice to terminate entailed legal sanctions, but it was still a choice. Since Roe v. Wade, those legal sanctions have been removed, but the choice remains a choice just as much as it ever was. Legislation, either for abortion or against abortion, does not remove the woman's free will, her ability to choose. The very existence of our legal system shows that people are always free to choose actions that are against the law, knowing that they will face consequences if they are caught. So we see that 'pro-choice' is a deceptive term; it is a mask for the term 'pro-abortion.' However, since most people do not want to appear to be actively and positively in favor of abortion, the more palatable term, 'pro-choice,' has become the preferred linguistic option.[3]

In contrast, the pro-life position affirms that all innocent life should be preserved and treated with dignity, with particular attention to those who are especially vulnerable: the unborn, the elderly, and the disabled. Sometimes abortion advocates challenge pro-life advocates about their support of mothers and of children after birth, accusing us of only caring about children in the womb. This is a fair challenge! Fortunately, most pro-life advocates are consistent in this matter, supporting mothers and families as well as protecting unborn children.[4]

SHIFTING MEANING

A more subtle form of manipulation comes from shifts in how a word is used, so that an assumption is buried in

---

[3] It is, however, becoming increasingly common to see direct 'pro-abortion' statements. Abortion is claimed as a positive good on the grounds that it protects the autonomy of the mother and enables her to engage in uncommitted sexual activity on an equal basis with men. The premise is that even if the unborn child is recognized as a human person, the mother's 'right' to autonomy has priority over the child's right to life. One contributing factor for the rise of this attitude may be a loss of robust meaning in our culture for the idea that the weak should be protected against the strong.

[4] For instance, the pro-life group Oxford Students for Life, at Oxford University, hosts talks and debates on a range of life issues, and advocates for support for student parents—an excellent example of a successful, and consistent, pro-life approach.

the meaning of the word, unnoticed by one of the parties. Unless the assumption is recognized and brought to light, the discussion can continue indefinitely on false premises. It's a form of equivocation—changing the terms of the argument midstream—but one that is particularly dangerous because it so often goes unobserved.

Consider 'marriage equality': here we have the most culturally transformative of all recent language shifts. The entire question of so-called 'gay marriage' hinges on the meaning of the word 'marriage'—but at a much more fundamental level than whether or not the definition of marriage stipulates a male-female union. The Catholic Church defines marriage as being between a man and a woman who freely give consent; it is characterized by fidelity, permanence, *and openness to children.*[5] This definition would until the 1930s have been shared by Protestants as well; this is not a merely Catholic position. It's important to note that we're talking about the *possibility* of children ('openness to' not 'procreation of'). A couple who are infertile, or who marry past the age of having children, are still in principle suited for child-bearing by their male-and-female complementarity, and by not contracepting they are showing their openness to life, even if in their particular case it doesn't happen. The same cannot be said about two men, or two women, for whom it is objectively impossible to conceive a child without another person of the opposite sex involved. The emotional com-

---

[5] See the *Catechism of the Catholic Church*, 1644–1654, 1662, 1664. Available online: <http://www.vatican.va/archive/ENG0015/_INDEX. HTM>.

ponent of marriage is important: the spouses are to love, care for, and support each other. However, it is only one part of the whole.

Once contraception was accepted as a legitimate, moral action, the culture's understanding of marriage lost one piece: openness to children. Thus, the popular definition of marriage now rests entirely on the emotional and social aspects of marriage. However, the *only* aspect of marriage that is *intrinsically* different for heterosexual couples is the ability, in principle, for the two partners, together, to conceive.[6] If openness to bearing children is an essential part of what it means to be married, then a gay couple obviously *cannot* be married. Note: not 'should not,' but 'cannot.' In contrast, if a marriage is based on two people providing emotional support for each other (with sexual activity as an aspect of emotional bonding, not as procreative), and if child-bearing is something that married couples may choose to do or not do as they wish, then it is very difficult to argue that a male-male or female-female relationship does not meet the same criteria for 'marriage' as a male-female contracepting relationship.

Thus, with the understanding of 'marriage' as meaning 'a socially sanctioned relationship between two people, based on their emotional bonding,' it is perfectly reason-

---

[6] The acceptance of sperm or egg donation and surrogacy also contributes to the breakdown of the concept of traditional marriage. In these cases of 'assisted' reproduction, a third person is involved. Even though adulterous intercourse does not take place, the act removes conception from its rightful context of the marital union, as an act of mutual self-giving. If a third person can be involved in the deepest mystery of a marriage, it becomes difficult in principle to argue that the matching of sexes in the married couple is particularly significant.

able to argue that proponents of traditional marriage are unfairly excluding people from a desirable status. In this curtailed view of what marriage is, favoring the male/female pairing in a marriage really is just a personal preference—or a prejudice. In the resulting cultural debate, the argument against 'gay marriage' is thus hamstrung from the start.

Another word that has undergone a subtle but massive shift is 'dignity.' For instance, the argument for assisted suicide as being 'death with dignity' is based on a very particular understanding of the meaning of 'dignity': that it means autonomy, the exercise of one's own will, and the avoidance of all physical or emotional pain. In this view, there is no place for dependence on others, and certainly no value in enduring suffering. This definition of 'dignity' is not universal. Someone who opposes assisted suicide, and who holds to a pro-life position, might well say: "I support death with dignity for everyone: I think that the elderly and terminally ill should be cared for, given the pain medication and palliative care that they need to be comfortable, and treated with respect; their dignity as human beings is inherent, not based on their ability to feed themselves or speak." However, that's a very different meaning of 'dignity' than intended in 'death with dignity'—where 'dignity' ought really to be translated as 'total personal autonomy and avoidance of pain.'

Here we see two hidden assumptions. One is that pain is to be avoided at all costs. Our culture is one in which people are terrified of suffering, and—in a very real way— would rather die than experience serious pain. As a result, the call to suffer with Christ in order to live with Christ is difficult for people to understand in a way it was not even fifty years ago. In order for much of Christian teaching and the witness of the saints to resonate with people, we need to reclaim the word 'dignity'—along with the redemptive value of suffering.

The other hidden assumption is that personal autonomy is the supreme value, the one that guides all other moral decisions. In this view, being able to choose for oneself outweighs the moral question of any particular choice. Since death is inevitable, it remains one of the fundamental givens of life; we cannot choose whether or not we will die, any more than we could choose for ourselves whether or not to be born. Such a lack of autonomy is, in this view, intolerable; at least suicide provides control over the time and manner of death. If the hidden assumption is brought to light, then we could have a worthwhile discussion: is the dignity of a human being dependent on personal autonomy? Is it inherently degrading to be cared for by another person? How do we rightly respond to the inevitability of death?

The significance of these hidden changes of meaning goes beyond their effect on our apologetics arguments. Once language becomes routinely distorted, it becomes increasingly easy to justify and promote evil—while at the same time hiding it behind positive words. Most people who support assisted suicide think that they are doing so for good reasons: eliminating suffering and providing the elderly and ill with control over their own lives. However, it is also rather uncomfortably true that this application of apparent mercy toward others is often very convenient for the survivors, who are thereby relieved of the burden of caring for the weak—either personally or corporately, as a society. Pope St. John Paul II, in his 1995 encyclical *Evangelium vitae*, writes:

> Even when not motivated by a selfish refusal to be burdened with the life of someone who is suffering, euthanasia must be called a false mercy, and indeed a disturbing "perversion" of mercy. True "compassion" leads to sharing another's pain; it does not kill the person whose suffering we cannot bear.[7]

Here it is important to note that a given person might use this perverted language of 'mercy killing' in an unreflective way. Take, for instance, the man who is caring for his elderly mother. Though he might honestly reject the idea that he wants his mother to die, the idea is still given a linguistic space in his mind, implicitly if not explicitly, by talk of 'assisting her to die with dignity': her living (and needing care) is not a simple fact of human life in relationship, but a situation caused by her own choice, and it is a choice which could be otherwise. Could her continued existence not begin to feel like an imposition to her or to him or to both of them? The very idea that her life need only last as long as she wants it to last, makes his caring for her contingent, provisional, and debatable, rather than absolute. She will be cared for as long as she wants to

---

[7] John Paul II, *Evangelium vitae*, 66. Available online: <http://w2.vatican.va/content/john-paul-ii/en/encyclicals/documents/hf_jp-ii_enc_25031995_evangelium-vitae.html>.

live; perhaps she might get tired of living and ask to be killed; perhaps everyone will be quietly relieved if she decides not to be a burden on anyone; perhaps hints could be dropped. . . .

LEGITIMIZATION

Another way in which language is distorted is through casual misuse. A word can become vitiated of meaning through too-broad application: consider, for instance, the way that the word 'awesome' has become for the most part a slangy synonym for 'very good' rather than meaning 'worthy of the response of awe.'

Too-broad usage of a word can also subtly shift our understanding of its core meaning. For instance, consider the adjectives 'hot' and 'sexy.' These have become a catch-all positive adjective, defying precise definition; certainly, they don't mean 'provoking sexual arousal,' or else descriptions of sexy cars and hot deals wouldn't make sense. The words do, however, have a sexual connotation, and they contribute to a general sense that sex is good, and that sex is everywhere and involved in everything. Even when applied more specifically to people, it's problematic.[8]

The casual use of 'hot' as an adjective of praise makes the language of sexual attraction into the default for describing attractiveness in general (and implies that physical beauty, as well as sex appeal, is the standard for beauty). When a man says "my lovely wife," he might mean

---

[8] Marc Barnes offers a brilliant takedown of the phrase "Modest is hottest" here: <http://www.patheos.com/blogs/badcatholic/2013/06/modest-is-not-hottest.html>.

that she is virtuous and hospitable, but "my hot wife" suggests a narrow set of physical characteristics, such as being fashionably dressed, carefully made-up, wrinkle-free, and above all *thin*. Language such as this is subversive of women's healthy self-image, even when it is accurate. It may be that the 'hot wife' is indeed thin and conventionally beautiful; will she still be 'hot' when her figure is no longer slim, or when she has wrinkles, gray hair, and hands crippled with arthritis? What about the woman who does not fit the Hollywood standard of beauty, and knows that she doesn't? She can be a good wife and a good mother, but if she is not actually physically attractive in the Hollywood sex-appeal kind of way, then the implication is "I praise you *as if* you were really beautiful, because it's unacceptable for you not to be sexy." The word 'hot,' like 'sexy,' drowns out other ways of praising a woman or man: virtuous, thoughtful, kind, devout, hospitable, a good mother, a good father. . . .

There is also the backwards legitimizing of the idea of pornography by applying 'porn' to innocent things: 'food porn,' for instance, for the enjoyment of looking at pictures of delicious meals. Corruption of language matters: imagine if the language of rape were applied to shopping, so people casually spoke of 'grocery rape.' That would be disgusting. The fact that 'food porn' is used as a humorous phrase means that the idea of pornography as a sin, as a degradation of the human being and a misuse of sex, has become lost.

Language matters, and one of the things that apologists must do is to be attentive to the way that language is used. We must ourselves be clear and use language well, and we must, as much as we can, challenge and resist the use of terms that cover up or distort the truth.

SYSTEMIC PROBLEMS

So far we've been discussing the distortion of language on the level of words and their meaning. However, there are also some deep-seated, systemic issues related to language that we must recognize and be prepared to deal with in our apologetics work.

The first systemic issue to consider is the excessive weight placed, in our modern culture, on the emotional effect of words and ideas. Words have great power, to hurt or heal, to break down or to build up, but the power itself is neutral. Some words are hurtful because they are false or demeaning, and encourage disrespect or even harmful actions; we are right to censure[9] these words. But other words hurt because they are true, and unwelcome in their truth (such as identifying masturbation or pre-marital sex as sins); or they create discomfort because they are new and challenging ideas that may cause us to stretch. A healthy culture censures the malicious use of language and encourages civility, while also recognizing that we cannot expect never to be challenged, uncomfortable, or even shocked. Unfortunately, our culture is not healthy.

This relentless focus on the emotional impact of ideas has the effect, among other things, of developing hyper-sensitivity in people in this environment, such that it becomes all the more difficult to present any idea that produces discomfort. We are seeing a trend toward the sup-

---

[9] Censure, not censor: a vital distinction!

pression of speech that makes anyone at all uncomfortable. The unfortunate truth is that more and more often, our Christian words and ideas shock, disturb, and unsettle the people who encounter them—and the response is to call for protection from hearing the ideas at all. It should not be so, but it is.

Language-policing is a move to avoid discussion or exploration of the truth or falsity of words that a group or individual doesn't like. It is often manipulative, and is a clever and unfortunately highly effective strategy to avoid having to make a counter-argument. Universities are increasingly adopting 'safe space' or 'no-platforming' policies to protect students from experiencing distress on account of hearing speech that they consider hurtful . . . with traditional Christian views on marriage, sexuality, gender identity, and the sanctity of life usually included on the list of offending ideas. The 'no-platforming' approach, in which certain points of view are simply banned from campus entirely, is more common in the U.K. at present, but it is likely that it will take root in the U.S. soon enough, given the tendency of students to protest speakers of whom they disapprove, and of administrations to be leery of bad publicity of any kind. The reason that 'safe space' and 'no-platforming' policies are so dangerous is that they move far beyond requiring people to be civil in their speech; rather, they impose the acceptance of a particular point of view by silencing the opposition. A classic example of 'no-platforming' was the 2014 shutdown of a scheduled debate at Oxford University; organized by Oxford Students for Life, the event would have featured a pro-choice and a pro-life speaker debating on the topic of 'Abortion Culture.' A women's group protested and threatened disruption; the hosting college withdrew permission for the event to be held in its lecture hall, citing safety issues; and the debate had to be cancelled.[10] Apologists should be prepared not just to defend their arguments, but also to defend the right to make those arguments in the first place.

Hyper-sensitivity has the further negative effect of often provoking people to speak deliberately in insulting or aggressive ways, out of frustration and annoyance with 'political correctness.' Neither suppression nor deliberate provocation is a healthy response—and the latter feeds into the former. However, we should not allow the excesses of emotion-based censorship to push us into being deliberately crass or insulting. The 'no platform' and 'safe space' strategies are effective because they can lay claim to part of the truth: that language can be used in ways that are hurtful and even destructive. There are words and phrases that we should avoid entirely, because they are demeaning, whether used intentionally to wound or simply with carelessness. Let me give one example: using the word 'vegetable' to refer to someone who is in a coma or has experienced severe brain damage. It's a word that reduces the person to an object and implicitly dismisses

---

[10] For more on this, see "Oxford cancels student-group-organized debate on abortion," *The Washington Post*, Nov. 19, 2014: <https://www.washingtonpost.com/news/volokh-conspiracy/wp/2014/11/19/oxford-cancels-student-group-organized-debate-on-abortion/> and the Oxford Students for Life blog: <https://blog.oxfordstudentsfor-life.co.uk/2014/11/20/our-debate-was-censored-this-week-heres-our-side-of-the-story/>

his or her humanity: not being able to move or speak does not make that person any less made in the image of God. Words like these are a sin against charity when used deliberately to wound or demean another, and any language that objectifies a person or reduces his or her humanity is wrong, even if that person doesn't notice or object.

There is no place in Christian communication for objectification of persons, for insults or for personal mockery. Unfortunately, it is necessary to make this point, because I have seen far too many examples of Christians, including apologists, failing in this regard: calling atheists 'idiots,' or worse. We must speak the truth, yes, and sometimes the truth will be difficult for our listeners to hear—but we must always speak with love and respect.

A second systemic problem is overstimulation. The media (including television, smartphones, and social media) has created an environment of constant overload of images, sound, information, and emotional response.[11] With so much to take in, much of it trivial but also distracting and addictive, it's difficult for people to discern what's important from what's not—and it's even more difficult for people to find the time and mental quietness necessary to really reflect on and take in the significance of what we say.

This overstimulation has contributed to the increasing cynicism and jadedness of the public about meaningful language in general, largely due to advertising: a veritable

---

[11] See, for instance, Neil Postman's illuminating *Amusing Ourselves to Death: Public Discourse in the Age of Show Business* (New York: Penguin, 1985), still relevant even though he wrote before the internet age.

tsunami of words and images that encourage the passive recipient to desire, buy, consume, desire more, buy more, consume more. Advertising-language is agenda-driven, and increasingly it's clear that media in general is designed to promote consumption. With product placement, sophisticated advertising, multimedia tie-ins, sponsored content, and so on, it is difficult not to be cynical about the claims being made in any media. We've all gotten used to the idea that everyone is trying to sell us something—but knowing this hasn't weakened the hold that advertisers have on us. Is it any wonder, then, that people are simultaneously deeply vulnerable to the effects of language and cynical about language?

One last difficulty to consider is that we do not have a shared culture to the extent that we did even fifty years ago, let alone further back. Our 'Christian language' was once known by most people, even if they did not accept our Faith, but now we speak a dialect—and one that has many local variations.

Human nature means that of course we're going to use language to mark our territories and define our tribes, as it were. When this tendency is kept in appropriate bounds, it's helpful in forming bonds of community. Having a 'dialect' for your community reaffirms the sense of belonging, and provides words for the sorts of things that perhaps the wider culture doesn't care about distinguishing. Just because a Protestant is unlikely to know that a 'novena' is a nine-day set of prayers, doesn't mean Catholics shouldn't use the term; just because a non-Christian would perhaps be baffled by the phrase 'Easter people,' we don't have to omit it from our vocabulary. We do, however, need to be aware of our audience, so that we can both make use of the richness of our Christian dialects in the appropriate context and communicate clearly to those who don't share the language of our community.

All told, we have a perfect storm of factors that make it difficult to talk seriously and fruitfully about our faith.

"Jesus Christ is Lord." How do people hear this?

*A power-claim—yet one more assertion of oppressive
    authority.*
Religious mumbo-jumbo. Meaningless.
*A threat. If this is true, it means that I must change
    my life.*
Personal opinion. If it works for you, great.
*A sales pitch. This isn't worth taking seriously:
    everybody is selling something. What are these
    Christians selling?*

We need to help our listeners realize that "Jesus Christ is Lord" means none of the above, but is rather a statement about the nature of reality: a truth that opens up the way to love, and hope, and joy. Apologetics means working to challenge and correct the many distortions and corruptions of language that get in the way of people understanding what we're saying.

UNMAKING LANGUAGE

'Repentance.' 'Virtue.' 'Sin': Words as relics
Of a weird, less sophisticated time,
A time that's wholly past and derelict,
Which we can only now bring back to mind
Enveloped in protective irony.
We've cordoned off our past and its 'concerns'
In the name of making us feel more free;
We *must* re-phrase—it's how our freedom's won.
And so we slice our bodies with no pain;
We grope in loveless sex with no release;
We search for self, though nothing there remains;
We make a ceaseless noise and find no peace.
Unmaking language, nothing left to say:
Blind impulse speaks, and wordless we obey.

CHAPTER FIVE

RECOVERY

WE have discussed the need to create a robust meaning for the words and ideas that we use in our apologetics work, considered the way that the imagination works in cooperation with the faculty of reason, and explored how figurative language can convey truth in different and complementary ways to literal language. We've also seen some of the ways that language is manipulated and distorted today, making the apologist's task much more difficult. In the next few chapters, we will apply these insights to specific areas where the imaginative apologist can get to work. We will consider what the issues are, and how the imaginative arts (literature in particular) can help.

To begin with, let's step back and look at the big picture.

What is the most important difference between the apologist and his audience? It is not merely that the apologist knows facts about God or Christian doctrine that the skeptical audience doesn't know (though this is often the case). It is that the Christian and the skeptic *have a different understanding of what they see.*

Many, if not most, non-Christians today find it difficult to 'see' Christianity as anything other than a cultural invention or purely subjective 'spiritual' experience. Popular culture, society, entertainment, and advertising—including the distracted mental environment of an always-on, media-saturated lifestyle—shape the way that people 'see' the Faith. Without realizing it, they have been taught (deliberately or not) that certain key concepts mean something other than what Christians mean by them. Faith is blind faith; God is a power-figure; reality equals the material world. This secularizing atmosphere is so pervasive that many Christians find it difficult to deepen or even to sustain their faith; it is one of the reasons that so many young people leave the Church when they go away to college. Not only are they exposed to more temptations or to direct atheist arguments (though this is also often the case), but these young people are now in an environment where many people 'see' the Faith as a superstition. Assumptions are harder to resist than arguments.

Owen Barfield writes that "wherever two consciousnesses differ, as it were, in kind, and not merely in relative lucidity—there the problem of sympathy can always be narrowed down to the meaning of some one or more fundamental words."[1] Using as his example Greek philosophy as read by modern Europeans, he notes that unless the reader "has enough imagination and enough power of detachment from the established meanings or thought-forms of his own civilization, to enable him to grasp the meaning of the fundamental terms . . . he will simply

[1] Barfield, *Poetic Diction*, 132.

re-interpret everything they say in terms of subsequent thought."[2] Speaking of his experiences in India, Andrew Davison notes that:

> People who believe in karma and reincarnation see a leper as someone paying the price for past sins. As a result they will not show him much pity. A Christian has a different worldview, and consequently sees the leper differently: as someone unfortunate, as someone requiring help. . . . The mental act of seeing already integrates sensation with value and meaning. We do not first see neutrally, and then interpret.[3]

We may not at first realize that people are doing this re-interpreting; they probably don't realize it themselves. But if we attend carefully to different perspectives, and find out where the real points of difference are, we have a much better chance of helping someone *see what we mean* —rather than simply repeating the same arguments that get re-interpreted in the same way.

Evangelical scholar Nancy Pearcey warns that in the study of worldviews, "It is all too easy to stick a label on an idea, slot it in the correct category, and then dismiss it without actively thinking it through. . . . The study of worldview and apologetics can descend into little more

---

[2] Ibid., 133.

[3] Andrew Davison, "Christian Reason and Christian Community," in *Imaginative Apologetics: Theology, Philosophy, and the Catholic Tradition*, ed. Andrew Davison (Grand Rapids, MI: Baker Academic, 2011), 15.

than a game of *Gotcha!* where winning the argument is all important."[4] In contrast, she suggests that "we demonstrate love for others when we study *their* worldview to get inside their thinking and find ways to connect God's truth with their innermost concerns and questions. . . . [We must] enter empathetically and compassionately into their experience of life."[5]

Such an entering-in on our part is necessary for us, not least because it allows us to discover the points of conflict that we are missing; it also helps us to discern how best to invite the skeptic (or the nominal Christian) into our way of seeing.

PERSPECTIVES

"I see what you mean" is an expression for "I understand," and for a good reason. Understanding is more than knowing facts; it requires putting those facts together and grasping their meaning. The skeptic, the believer of another religion, and the spiritual-but-not-religious person may have the same facts before them as the Christian, but they won't necessarily put them together in the same way. If we recognize this, we can steer clear of a great deal of unnecessary frustration, resist the temptation to believe that our interlocutors are stupid or willfully blind, and instead address the larger issue.

We always necessarily understand what we see through our own perspective. Contra the claims of modernism, we

---

[4] Nancy Pearcey, *Saving Leonardo: A Call to Resist the Secular Assault on Mind, Morals, & Meaning* (Nashville, TN: B&H, 2010), 17–18.

[5] Ibid., 18.

cannot inhabit a neutral, 'outside' perspective, as if we could look at God from outside of him. That's impossible, for to be outside of him, the Ground of All Being, is not to exist at all. Indeed, the idea that total detachment is possible is itself a perspective, one that denies the incarnational reality of ourselves as human beings (body and soul) who have a lived history that actually matters. In this light, it is worth reflecting on the fact that Our Lord chose to go through the entire process of human life, beginning with conception and growth in Mary's womb: his Incarnation is not as Everyman but as one man, the son of Mary, the foster son of Joseph, the carpenter from Nazareth.

However, contra some forms of postmodernism, we are not trapped in our subjective perspective, nor are all perspectives equally valid.[6] There *is* objective reality, and our perspective may or may not be fully in line with it. Just as we must reject the impossible task of gaining an outside, 'objective' view, we must also reject the claim that we are stuck in our own perspective, and that the step from one worldview to another must be entirely blind, because it is all or nothing.

Christians too often get tangled up by fears of relativism whenever the idea of perspectives is raised, as if the only alternatives were disembodied objectivity on the one hand and total relativism on the other.[7] That's a false

---

[6] And, contra some versions of presuppositional apologetics, we can engage with alternative perspectives, and are not reduced to merely asserting the Christian one.

[7] For instance, Alasdair MacIntyre is too often accused of relativism in his work *After Virtue*, even though he specifically states that he is not a relativist, and though the work itself is an extended (albeit subtle

dichotomy. Let me say at the outset that when I talk about different perspectives, I am not ceding any ground whatsoever to relativism.

Consider this example. I am very near-sighted and have been all my life. When I was a little girl, though, the soft and blurry way I saw the world seemed simply to be the way the world is, and so it didn't occur to me to speak up about it. Only when I went to school did I realize that things were different for my classmates: for them, the faint smudges of white on the blackboard could be seen as distinct shapes and letters from all the way at the back of the class! By observing others, I discovered that their perception of the world was not quite the same as mine—and that mine could be corrected. In the space between realizing I needed glasses, and getting them, I realized that there *was* a different way of looking at the world, and that it would be better, although I did not (and could not) yet know what it would be *like*. Then, when I got glasses for the first time, I entered fully into a new way of seeing. However, the process of getting my prescription right wasn't smooth. One set of glasses caused me to see double, and despite the doctor's claim that I would soon get used to them, I didn't. Fortunately, the next attempt was more successful.

But how did I *know* that my first set of glasses wasn't right? After all, I was moving from one perspective (blurry, nearsighted vision) to another that I had never experienced. Might it not be the case that clarity of vision is necessarily

---

and complex) examination of how one can assess different perspectives.

accompanied by headaches and double vision? No: I realized that this alternative perspective, though it was an improvement in some ways, was still *not right*. I could tell both from my own discomfort and inner sense of wrongness, and from the testimony of people I trusted, who assured me that wearing glasses should be comfortable.

So, we see from a certain perspective, but we are not limited by it. Our context is our home, not our prison; we can venture outside. Through the God-given faculty of imagination, we can enter into other perspectives, and through the faculty of reason, we can assess the truth or falsity of what we discover.

A holistic, fully-integrated approach to apologetics helps people to make both those moves: first to enter into the Christian perspective, and then to recognize it as true. What might that entail? We will consider three points as we explore this question: 1) seeing things in right relation; 2) seeing clearly; 3) seeing things as a whole.

SEEING THINGS IN RIGHT RELATION

Our Christian faith is not just a theological system that is overlaid on an otherwise unrelated material world. Rather, the Faith encompasses all of reality—spiritual, mental, material, emotional. Everything fits together. This is, I would suggest, the most convincing argument for the Faith: that everything coheres. It is the explanatory model par excellence, the key that opens all the doors of the universe.

Thus, we should have, as a long-term apologetics strategy, the aim of showing how everything fits together in our Faith: how everything that we believe helps us to understand everything else. In short, our Faith gives us a truly three-dimensional view of the world, with everything in right *relation* to everything else.

Each of us relates to friends and loved ones in a subjective way—in the light of all our shared experiences, the friendship and love we have for each other, the bond of commitments made and hope for the future. A man of integrity will display his character consistently in all of his relationships, but he will be 'seen' differently from the perspectives of other people: his own father and mother, his brothers and sisters, his wife, his children, his friends, colleagues, fellow parishioners, and so on . . . and this is as it should be.

Likewise, all truth is perceived in *relation* to other truths. I understand who I am as a person, relative to my family, my friends, my colleagues, and so on. When I learn something new about the Faith or grow in my prayer life, the new insight does not stand by itself, but is perceived and assimilated in relation to other things that I already know and have experienced. When I first became a Christian, and later when I first entered the Catholic Church, this process of growth included times when the new insight, the newly grasped truth, showed the error or weakness of other ideas or habits—in *relation* to them—and so I experienced conviction of sin, awareness of weakness, and the need to reject certain ideas and habits of mind. The resulting changes might not be externally dramatic, but they nonetheless represented real and sometimes painful growth. For instance, I realized that being truly charitable involves giving more than what is easy to give, and that financial security is good, but not as an end in itself. Likewise, I have come to see that being part of the Church means that I, a shy and reserved introvert, must stretch beyond what's always comfortable for me in order to be part of the community.

In fact, it is essential for someone to grasp an idea *relative to* other beliefs and practices he or she may hold: only then can that person truly accept or reject it, and grow. If an idea is held in a kind of hermetically sealed container, touching nothing and affecting nothing in ourselves, then it cannot be said to have been fully understood. But if a person is able to see how an idea relates meaningfully with all his other ideas, each idea will make more sense and be more meaningful than on its own.

SEEING CLEARLY

C. S. Lewis shows in his essay "Bluspels and Flalansferes" that the faculty of reason depends upon the faculty of imagination to give it meaningful things to reason *about*.[8] As we have seen, even straightforward explanations and arguments can be obscured by assumptions and misinterpretations, or affected by distortion or the corruption of language. The words that we use to talk about the Faith are rich with meaning, but that meaning is often not accessible to the people we're speaking with (even when those people are fellow Christians). We can, and must, ask, "What do you mean by that?" The defining of terms is essential and must consciously be attended to in apologetics and evangelism.

---

[8]   See C. S. Lewis, "Bluspels and Flalansferes: A Semantic Nightmare," in *Selected Literary Essays*.

But our imaginative vision must be healthy and functioning as well, or our reason will not have the proper materials with which to work. It's all very well to talk about considering different perspectives, but as part of that, we must see clearly—or else what we see will be distorted by our own assumptions and misunderstandings.

J. R. R. Tolkien gives us a sketch of how imaginative literature can help. He argues that one of the functions of fantasy literature is what he calls Recovery, a "regaining of a clear view," going on to say, "I do not say 'seeing things as they are' and involve myself with the philosophers, though I might venture to say 'seeing things as we are (or were) meant to see them'—as things apart from ourselves."[9]

Tolkien identifies two related elements that contribute to our failure to see clearly: familiarity and possessiveness. Using the metaphor of a dirty, smudged window—whose film of grime obscures what we see through it—he says that we need "to clean our windows; so that the things seen clearly may be freed from the drab blur of triteness or familiarity—from possessiveness."[10] This analysis is of the utmost importance for apologetics. We live in a culture that is paradoxically both jaded by and ignorant about Christianity. People think they know who Jesus is, what the Church is, what it means to have faith . . . and they think it's boring, or stupid, or irrelevant. We need to help people recover a fresh view of the truth—to see Jesus for the first time, and really see him; to actually

[9] Tolkien, "On Fairy-stories," 67.
[10] Ibid.

see the reality of sin, and the beauty and brokenness of the world, not to just gloss over it.

Someone who is convinced that 'God' means 'old man in the sky' is quite right to consider it ridiculous; to that person, arguments for the existence of an old man in the sky are self-evidently false, worthy only of mockery. Now, this atheist needs to realize that Christians do not simply believe in one sky-father figure out of many options (as opposed to, say, Zeus) but that the word 'God' means, to us, 'the Ground of All Being': God is existence itself or as he says to Moses, "I AM."[11] However, if our young atheist is already convinced that he knows what God means, he's not going to pay much attention to attempts to correct his misunderstanding. What he needs is to see the idea afresh.

Stories can help us to do that. For example, consider how a reader can be drawn into Tolkien's world of Middle-earth. After reading about the Ents, Tree-beard and the other shepherds of the trees, we can look at an ordinary tree, a pine or oak, and think: how extraordinary, really, is a tree! Perhaps we will think differently about efforts to protect the environment, or plant more trees in our cities and towns. We can be moved by the self-sacrifice of Frodo and the kingliness of Aragorn and thus respond more immediately, more intuitively, to these ideas when we hear them in the Gospel. Good stories and poetry help us to see more clearly when we close the book and re-enter ordinary life.

We need stories that allow people (Christians as much as non-Christians) to recognize the potential to be made

[11] Exodus 3:14.

whole in their own lives: for marriages, families, and friendships to be healthy and shaped as God made them to be; for our 'daily bread' to be tasted and savored once again; for the possibility of divine love and forgiveness.

Jesus said that unless we become like little children, we cannot enter the Kingdom of Heaven. Part of being childlike is to see things afresh: to look at God's creation and see it as his handiwork, to be able to read the words of Holy Scripture and be deeply moved at what we find.

SEEING THINGS AS A WHOLE

But there is a third piece to the puzzle. We cannot see rightly if we see things in isolation. Our Faith is not a set of isolated propositions, each of which can be assented to separately. It is an integrated whole. To say "God, the Holy Trinity, exists" is a different kind of claim than saying "Winston Churchill existed." We are making a claim about the nature of reality, not about one more object that is included in the cosmos.

And so before we even address issues such as "Did the Resurrection really happen?" or "Are miracles possible?" or "What is the Church?" or "Is the Bible true?", we have a larger question, often unspoken but vitally important for our modern audience: what is the nature of reality?

To put it more precisely, we need first to ask if it is possible for the *unseen* to be real. Is there a supernatural dimension to reality, or is the material world—that which we see, hear, touch, smell, and taste—all that there is?

This is not to say that all apologetics discussions must go in a certain sequence, starting with questions of naturalism and supernaturalism before addressing any other topic. Not at all: for one thing, conversations can go in more than one direction (and usually go back and forth!). What I am suggesting, rather, is that the way people react to, and deal with, the claims of Christianity is conditioned by their overall view of the way the world works. If there is no supernatural element in a person's understanding of the world—if, on the practical level, he or she views the world in a purely naturalistic light, as a closed system— then most of the ideas central to Christianity will have no traction whatsoever. They will be puzzling, perhaps, but only in the "Huh, that's kind of weird" way.

Why is the reality of the supernatural such a vital point? Consider this analogy.

Most people today recognize that vitamins are important for health. Imagine that you've been experiencing fatigue. A friend suggests that perhaps you have a vitamin deficiency, and sends you some articles to read. Most of the articles are from sites you think might be biased (because they sell vitamins), but still, the points they're making are reasonable, and you've been able to follow up on a few of the claims with other sources. You decide that it's worth taking a vitamin supplement for a while. Of course you know it won't have instant results, so you decide to try it for six months and see if it makes a difference.

Reasonable, right?

Now imagine that your friend, instead of suggesting vitamins, argues that really the problem is the color of your clothes. You're wearing the wrong colors on the wrong days of the week. She sends you articles arguing that colors are actually the result of an intersection with a fifth dimension (which we perceive as color), and the colors we wear either sustain or disrupt our alignment with that dimension. Following a particular system of matching your clothing color with the day of the week will put you back into harmony. Why not try it? In one sense, it's easier than the vitamin option, since it won't cost you anything. You don't even need to buy any new clothes, just make different choices about when to wear certain colors (and don't, under any circumstances, wear stripes).

Would you try it? I would venture to suggest that you probably would not, and for good reason. It sounds daft. (It *is* daft.) The whole idea is based on claims that are contrary to what you know about science. You'd be embarrassed to even suggest that you think it might be true. Fifth-dimensional colors are not part of the world as you understand it.

Now imagine that you are entirely confident that the physical world is *all that there is*: that the mind is the same thing as the brain, that there is no such thing as a soul, that 'miracle' is another name for 'coincidence,' and that your consciousness will simply switch off at death. And then imagine that someone tells you: "A man who died two thousand years ago loves you and wants you to live forever with him."

Right.

Now, there are lots of ways to help people get past the weirdness of talking about Jesus as a living person whom we can get to know. One of them is the existence of the Church, and another is the long list of highly intelligent and well-educated people of different personalities, cultures, and times who have considered this claim about Jesus to be rational and true. However, these approaches aren't as effective as they used to be, because people today are increasingly less informed about history, especially the history of the Church, and are ever more bombarded with anti-Christian and anti-Catholic propaganda. We have to assume that most people know practically nothing about Christianity or its contribution to culture, and that much of what they think they know is completely false.[12]

In short, we have a lot of work to do. Not only do we need to make good arguments, but we need to help shape the underlying assumptions and views that people have, so that they take our arguments seriously—so that the words we use have meaning and aren't just tokens in a game of atheist vs. Christian.

We need to enlarge the field of view. We can tackle the worldview question directly, by working on the assumptions that people hold, and showing that the intellectual framework of naturalism doesn't stand up to the weight of reality. But we can also use smaller arguments and ideas to do some of the work as well. A specific instance of something that doesn't fit into the naturalistic worldview (historical evidence for the Resurrection; miracles of healing; even something as small as the incorrupt bodies of certain saints) can lead a skeptic to reconsider whether his worldview is big enough to account for all of reality.

---

[12] A helpful resource is *Bearing False Witness: Debunking Centuries of Anti-Catholic History* (West Conshohocken, PA: Templeton Press, 2016) by Rodney Stark, a Protestant historian.

A HOLISTIC VISION

Here, we must take a careful, searching look at our own beliefs and how we act on them. Given the cultural pressures from reductive scientism and naturalism, and the relentless materialism of our consumer culture, it is very easy (and all too common) even for well-discipled Christians to have a somewhat impoverished worldview. Many Christians tend to think of the supernatural realm as including only God and nothing more—and in such a view, 'God' often ends up being seen as not particularly supernatural either.

But the full Christian view is of a dynamic cosmos: with the communion of saints, the great "cloud of witnesses,"[13] actively interested in the affairs of their brothers and sisters and interceding for them; angels who are active in God's service; demons who are active in rebellion; and the network of connections formed by prayer and intercession among Christians.

This is the dynamic world of Catholic faith. How much poorer we are when we lose sight of it!

We've imbibed far too much of the modernist, skeptical, naturalistic ethos. It's as if we're trying to reduce the supernatural to the smallest amount possible, the least complex system we can think of, in order to make it more believable or palatable. It's simpler, right? Catholic worship and devotion often seems strangely complex to those on the outside. Can't we just believe in Jesus? Certainly, we must come to the Father like little children—but to have faith that is child*like* is not the same as faith that

---

[13] Hebrews 12:1.

is child*ish*—and the fact that one can trust on the basis of very little knowledge is not an adequate argument for ceasing to grow in knowledge. A child's level of understanding does not set a limit to the complexity of reality.

Consider the interrelations of an ecosystem: a coral reef, a marshland, a hedgerow, even a simple field. Consider the complexity of the human body; the genome; the amazing intricacies of a single cell. All this, God made. If he made the physical world to be so complex, so richly inter-related and dynamic, then what basis is there for assuming that the spiritual world is simple and one-dimensional?

It is, indeed, more complex to believe that those who die in friendship with God spend time being purified of the effects of their sin, that they are helped in this purification by the prayers of their loved ones, and that, once they are through Purgatory, that they, in turn, can intercede in prayer for their loved ones still on Earth. It's simpler to imagine that there's no purgatorial step. But simplification doesn't mean truth, in and of itself: it's even simpler to make the universalist claim and say that there's only one destination for every soul, and that rather than two ultimate destinies, hell and heaven, there's only one. Or, for the naturalistic version of universalism, that the ultimate destiny for every person is extinction and decay. Simpler? Yes. True? No.

In our own experiences, reality is complex. So if it's complex on the physical level, why *not* on the spiritual? If we can help people to see that as a possibility, then the world that is described in Holy Scripture begins to seem much less alien, much more of a description of reality.

Thus, an important part of our apologetics endeavor

is an attempt to help people see things differently. Seeing differently is not the same thing as believing; but it is a step in the right direction.

A SUDDEN GOLDFINCH

The branch is bare and black against the fog;
Cold droplets bead along the twigs, and fall.
The hours are passing, ready to be gone,
And now they're past, dissolved, beyond recall,
Beyond my reach. A sudden goldfinch clings
And bends the twig so slightly with its weight
It seems as if it's painted on: its wings
In motion are a glimpse of summer, bright,
Quick, and now already gone. This moment,
So brief but still so clear against the blur
Of unattended time, in memory
Connects the things that are, the things that were.
Fleeting as it is, almost a ghost,
It may be time is never truly lost.

CHAPTER SIX

The Incarnation

The Incarnation of Christ is at the heart of our Christian faith. Every other doctrine depends on this: that Jesus of Nazareth is fully God and fully man. Without the Incarnation, there can be no salvation. Without Jesus having a fully human body, from Mary's own flesh and blood, there would have been no real death on the Cross, and no bodily resurrection on the third day; the Resurrection as a historical, and not merely 'spiritual,' event depends on the reality of the Incarnation. Only if Jesus is fully man could he unite himself fully with us, and suffer death on the Cross; only if Jesus is fully God could he redeem this human nature with his death.

Here is the deepest and most life-giving paradox of faith: that the One by whom all things were made condescended to enter into the messy, sinful world of ordinary men and women. The etymology of 'condescend' underscores the meaning of the Incarnation: from the Latin, 'together' (*com*) and 'descend' (*descendere*), Our Lord came down from Heaven to be together with us in our humanity. He limited himself; he chose freely to make himself weak and vulnerable, and to suffer *with* us so that he could suffer and die *for* us.

What's more, the Incarnation sanctifies all stages of life, and sanctifies the family; Our Lord is truly like us in all things but sin. As Oxford's Fr. John Saward writes:

> In the womb of the Blessed Virgin, God the Son, without ceasing to be true and perfect God, was made true and perfect man, a real and complete human being. . . . He could have created for Himself a human body in adult form, as He did for Adam, but such was not His will. . . . By the wise and merciful decree of the Trinity, the Son took the slow way into the world of men, the low road of childhood; He chose to be mothered into humanity. Thus, for Him, as for us, the beginning of human life was conception in a mother's womb, though in His case the Mother was a virgin, and the active principle of the conception was not the material seed of any man but the immaterial Spirit of God. . . . Having been conceived, the Incarnate Word remained for a full nine months within His Mother's body, and then he came forth, again in a miraculous manner, but with all the essential littleness and weakness of infancy to human eyes displayed.[1]

Because the Incarnation is central to our Faith, we should consider how to make it central to our apologetics

---

[1] Fr. John Saward, *Cradle of Redeeming Love: The Theology of the Christmas Mystery* (San Francisco: Ignatius Press, 2002), 157–158.

as well. The Incarnation has implications both for *what* we say in our apologetics and *how* we say it.

That the Word became flesh has implications for all aspects of life, including our self-understanding, our relationships with others, and how we relate to the created world. The Christian hope is for a renewal of all Creation; the future we anticipate is not a disembodied spirit-heaven, but rather "a new heaven and a new earth."[2] From the very beginning, God's plan included our human bodies and the physical world that we live in. God made Adam and Eve before the Fall; their embodied-ness was not a mistake or a consequence of sin, but our intended state. We see a reminder of this in the too-often overlooked event of Jesus's Ascension: although the Incarnation of Christ had a beginning, at his conception in Mary's womb, it does not have an end. Jesus was raised bodily from the dead, and ascended into heaven, still in the flesh; glorified in his Resurrection body. The Son of God is now, and forever, incarnate; humanity has been brought into the Trinity. We are not just souls that happen to have bodies; we are embodied souls, or ensouled bodies.[3] When we die, our souls are separated from our bodies, but this is only a temporary state: we who die in friendship with Christ can look forward to the fact that on the Last Day, our bod-

---

[2] Revelation 21:1.

[3] Let me take a moment to point out a frequent misattribution to C. S. Lewis. The line "You are not a body, you are a soul; you have a body" was *never* said by Lewis, and indeed with its implicit Gnosticism is counter to Lewis's theology. William O'Flaherty has an excellent series of articles confirming Lewis quotes and revealing fakes, here: <http://www.essentialcslewis.com/confirming-c-s-lewis-quotations-series-overview/>.

ies will be restored to us, resurrected and glorified. God has even underscored the permanently embodied nature of our humanity by the bodily assumption of three human beings into heaven: the prophets Enoch and Elijah, and the Blessed Virgin Mary.

God made all that is, and called it good. Human beings are responsible for the world being broken, but God did not therefore declare that he would get rid of it; rather, he declared his plan to redeem it. As part of his life and ministry, Our Lord forever sanctified material things; he made the world sacramental. When he was baptized by John, Our Lord sanctified water itself. In his first miracle, at the wedding at Cana, Our Lord turned water into wine—a miracle involving material things, wine to drink at a party. In the Eucharist, he gives us his own body and his own blood for our salvation.

One of the strengths of imaginative apologetics is that it can be strongly incarnational, thus providing an important complement to more purely abstract or analytical arguments for the Faith. The arts have a significant role to play in this incarnational approach. Music and the visual arts are also vitally important, but here I will discuss only literature, in part because it is my field and the area that I love, but also because it can claim a certain priority over the other arts: there is something special about language. We have revelation through inspired human words in Holy Scripture and, pre-eminently, in God's perfect and complete self-revelation in the Word made flesh, Our Lord Jesus Christ.

EMOTIONS

Human emotions are part of the experience of being embodied, and demonstrate the interconnectedness of mind, spirit, body. Sorrow may be experienced as a tightness in the throat, a knot in the stomach, or a heaviness in the limbs; love, as a feeling of lightness, the heart beating faster, a thrill in the nerves, or a feeling of warmth. While emotions can lead us astray (in our fallen state), the human capacity for emotion is itself good, not sinful. The Gospel accounts show us that Jesus felt emotions, giving us a glimpse of his expressions of sorrow and love. We see, for instance, in the Gospel of John, that Jesus has a deep friendship with Martha, Mary, and Lazarus; when he saw Mary mourning for her dead brother, "he was greatly disturbed in spirit and deeply moved"[4] and indeed wept for Lazarus himself.

In a rightly ordered human being, rational understanding is accompanied by appropriate emotional response: St. Paul directs us to rejoice with those who rejoice and weep with those who weep.[5] We feel most acutely for those who are close to us personally, as it's fitting and good for us to do, but if our emotions are ordered rightly, we will also feel an emotional response in some degree to the terrible tragedies and great goods that happen to others, far away.

One of the characteristics that makes literature incarnational is that it has the power to evoke emotion in the reader. Readers may experience sympathy or dislike for characters in a novel; suspense or excitement at the un-

---

4 John 11:28–36.
5 Romans 12:15.

folding of a plot; joy or melancholy when reading poetry.

Literature's power of prompting an emotional reaction is in itself neutral. To be sure, authors can use the power of language and storytelling to make evil things seem harmless, normal, or even appealing; emotion can be evoked in the cause of wickedness. But language and images can always be manipulated such as to mislead or produce a response that is not in line with the good. (Consider pornography, or the manipulation of love for family or nation to sell merchandise.) Emotional response to the images we see and the language we hear and read is an innate part of being human; people are not, never will be, and indeed cannot be purely rational and un-affected by emotion. Indeed, if they were, they would have ceased to be fully human.

Literature offers a mode of apologetics in which we can guide the natural human emotional response toward its right end, by presenting truth in such a way that we are moved on the level of our emotions as well as convinced on the level of our intellect. When emotion and intellect are in line, rather than at odds, with each other and both are oriented toward the good, then it becomes easier for the will to direct action toward the good.

NARRATIVE

Narrative provides another incarnational mode of apologetics. While there are non-narrative forms of literature, there is often a hint of implicit story even in a primarily lyric poem or in a predominantly character-focused drama.

As we have seen earlier in this book, we have an innate need for meaning in our lives. Because we are creatures who inhabit time and—importantly—who perceive the passing of time, we need to have this meaning expressed in a fundamentally narrative form. The unstated default expectation of human beings is that our lives have a beginning, a middle, and an end that relate to each other in an intelligible way: random acts and events are distressing, and have to be integrated into our lives, often with real effort.

As a result, we are naturally predisposed to take in truth in the form of narrative, and to use narrative forms to reflect on, process, and act on those truth claims. It's worth noting that non-linear narrative techniques are ancient and well-established: consider, for instance, Homer's *Odyssey*, which begins in the middle of the story and fills out the details with extended flashbacks. Such a structure is actually based on our expectation of a meaningful narrative: we understand that the pieces are out of order, and we enjoy fitting the pieces into place and understanding the full picture. In fact, the mental experience of making meaning from the narrative elements ("Oh, so that's why . . .") echoes and reinforces the ongoing discovery of meaning in our own lives.

The best indication of this innate human disposition toward narrative is that much of Scripture is in this form. The Scriptures could, if God had so intended, been inspired in such a way that the human authors would have written a purely propositional book, with doctrine and guidelines for behavior. Instead, much of the revelation of God is presented through narrative. In the Old Testament, the Law is not given in isolation, but is part of the story of the Israelites, first in slavery under Pharaoh, then led by Moses to freedom, followed by the years in the desert on the way to the Promised Land. The story of the Exodus is equally as inspired as the Ten Commandments. The Gospels include Jesus's direct moral teaching, as with the Sermon on the Mount, but they include far more narrative of his life: his birth, his interactions with people during his ministry, the miracles that he performed, and the events of his Passion, death, and Resurrection.

Using narrative in apologetics allows the apologist to embody abstract truth in a story that the reader or listener can engage with. The direct use of literature, drama, and film, through shared reading, performing, or viewing (and subsequent discussion), is one way to incorporate narrative into apologetics, but there are other ways to make use of it as well.

First, Scripture and theology can be taught in the context of the larger story of God's involvement with human history. As one example, the doctrine of the Trinity can be embedded in the context of Jesus's baptism in the River Jordan, where, as the Son comes up from the water, the Holy Spirit alights upon him like a dove, and the Father speaks from Heaven to say "This is my Son, the Beloved, with whom I am well pleased."[6] The scene is vivid and makes the distinction of the three Persons of the Trinity memorable. Teaching on the attributes of God will be much more effective if it is grounded in stories from Scripture that demonstrate these attributes as God interacts with his people. Such an approach moves beyond using individual verses and passages as proof-texts and

[6]   Matthew 3:13–17.

engaging with them in greater depth, allowing people to experience the fullness of what Scripture means.

Second, teaching itself can draw on the nature of story. We like conflict, suspense, and resolution in our stories; a speaker or teacher can set the stage for a lecture or discussion with intellectual, theological, or moral conflicts and suspense. This approach is more engaging to the audience, who can follow the 'story' of the unfolding argument or lesson.

Third, we can draw much more on Church history and on the lives of the saints in general apologetics. Many of the challenges we face today have been faced by Christians in centuries past; often the perceived distance provided by history allows for a fresh perspective on a subject. The history of the Church itself is extremely exciting—as someone said, the existence of the Church is itself an argument for the truth of Christianity—and, properly told, knocks out some of the typical claims against Christianity, such as it being anti-science or anti-woman. The lives of the saints through the past two thousand years provide another form of apologetics. It is difficult to imagine that anything other than a genuinely true religion could inspire people from so many different cultures, times, walks of life, and personalities to become Christians and to love and serve Our Lord with all their might. Because the saints are so varied, and so interesting, their lives are a cultural apologetic against the secular assumption that heaven is a boring place where you sit on a cloud and play a harp, and that being good and moral is a dull business. The saints also offer a point of entry, as it were: examples of conspicuous holiness and goodness (even by secular standards) that draw the attention, and may help people to wonder: what motivated that person? How could I gain some of that joy, some of that strength?

SPECIFICITY

A third incarnational aspect of imaginative apologetics is its *specificity*. An idea that can be expressed proposition-ally can potentially be expressed in an infinite number of ways: "It is not good for man to be alone" provides the foundation for any number of romances. The idea is em-bodied in particular details: this character, this location, this sequence of events, these colors and shapes. By the very limitation inherent in these specific choices of story, characters, and images, the truth becomes tangible, and thus more accessible and more engaging.

Using stories and art to embody doctrine (as well as explaining it) is particularly useful for combating gnos-ticism—a pervasive heresy that affects Christians as well as non-Christians. The gnostic view is that the spiritual is all that's truly real or important; the material is unreal or unimportant. Thus, gnosticism proposes that we can do whatever we like with our bodies, either using them for sensual pleasure (hence, hedonism and libertinism) or striving to purify them and bring them to a state of per-fection (hence, obsessions with 'eating clean' and weight loss). Oddly, even dyed-in-the-wool materialist skeptics often have a broad streak of gnosticism. They may con-cede that God might possibly exist, as a sort of spiritual force, but that *if* he exists, he certainly would not do any-thing as crass as to have been gestated in a woman's body for nine months and be born.

One of the great evangelistic mistakes of the nineteenth and early twentieth Century was the capitulation to modernism among many preachers and teachers, under the mistaken idea that it would be easier for people to accept Christianity as primarily an ethical system, without the messy bits of the Incarnation and Resurrection as historical events and without strange things like miracles. In fact, this approach made it easier for people to reject the Faith. Today, we must deal with the ongoing consequences of this great error; we must help people to understand that Christian faith is not simply assent to certain ethical precepts (important as that is) but that it means entering into relationship with a living, fully embodied person— Our Lord Jesus Christ, Son of God and Son of Mary.

Holy Scripture is specific in precisely this way: we discover that God has interacted, and continues to interact, with the material world in ways that are often very surprising to us, and involving all kinds of people: men and women, young and old, rich and poor; the brave and the shy, the eloquent and the mute; farmers, poets, servants, soldiers, bureaucrats, kings, shepherds. . . . One of the tasks of imaginative apologetics is to create, and share, stories and images that present our Faith in specific terms: vivid, compelling, embodied.

By being specific, stories also have the merit of being relational—as is our Faith. Literature, through image and metaphor, offers ways of encountering truth that are fundamentally open-ended. To say that Christ is the morning star[7] is a metaphor that can be unpacked in a

---

[7] Revelation 22:16.

variety of ways: he lights the way, he is the firstborn of all creation, he is beautiful, and so on. But the image itself means more than any of the ways that we would translate it into propositional language. It creates a space for reflecting on who Christ is, and where the reader is in relation to him.

Story, narrative, is also incomplete; all stories that an author tells must come to an end, but life goes on. The reader can imagine the characters still carrying on with new adventures that are unrecorded by the author's pen, and the reader can imagine himself or herself into the story. Furthermore, every story has details that are not described by the author, but can be imagined by the reader. The more vividly realized the world of the story, the more likely it is that the reader will want to 'inhabit' that story and experience it imaginatively. The reader's response is part of the experience; there is always more to be understood, more to be engaged with. A story that conveys truth and beauty will show more of its truth and beauty each time the reader comes to it, and in a different way, because the reader will be different, coming to the text with new experiences, different moods, different questions.

THEORY OF MIND

Finally, one incarnational aspect of literature that is particularly valuable for apologists is that it helps readers develop a robust *theory of mind*: the ability to imagine what another person is thinking or feeling. On a relational and moral level, having a well-developed theory of mind is vital: it enables us to see the other person truly as other, separate and different from ourselves, with their own thoughts, feelings, experiences, and sense of self. While having a strong theory of mind does not in itself guarantee that the person will then be empathetic and compassionate, it makes stronger empathy and compassion possible.

Since it is only possible to experience one self (our own), all exercise of theory of mind must be done through the imagination, putting together what we know and have observed about someone else to develop an idea about what his or her personal experience is like. Our own experiences are an important starting point. For instance, as a convert to Christianity from atheism, I know that it can be frightening to seriously consider such a radical change in one's beliefs. As a result, I can imagine multiple reasons why an atheist might behave in a defensive manner or choose to end a discussion, and recognize that the conversation may still have been highly productive. However, personal experience is by its very nature sharply limited: I don't know what it's like, firsthand, to have doubts about faith while growing up in a Christian family. In order to be effective as an apologist, I need to be able to empathize with those whose experiences I have not shared.

Literature is extremely helpful in this regard for both deepening and broadening one's theory of mind. To begin with, reading imaginative fiction that focuses on character development and interaction, such as the fiction of Jane Austen[8] or Anthony Trollope, helps us hone the skills of observing others, drawing conclusions about

[8] See, for instance, this excellent blog post on Jane Austen: "Why Every Man Should Read Jane Austen," at *The Art of Manliness*: <http://www.artofmanliness.com/2016/06/27/why-every-man-should-read-jane-austen/>.

their character, reactions, and intentions, and then testing those conclusions.

Good stories do more than allow us to practice theory of mind: they also give us more material with which to work. Literature, here including both fiction and non-fiction in the form of well-written memoirs and biographies, can help us to see from another's perspective. We have the opportunity to experience other cultures and times, to learn from other experiences, and to engage the world through a different personality, perhaps even very different values and ideas. As Lewis says in *An Experiment in Criticism*: "Literary experience heals the wound, without undermining the privilege, of individuality. . . . in reading great literature I become a thousand men and yet remain myself. Like the night sky in the Greek poem, I see with a myriad eyes, but it is still I who see. Here, as in worship, in love, in moral action, and in knowing, I transcend myself; and am never more myself than when I do."[9]

For the apologist, these literary experiences help develop our ability to realize that a truth that seems obvious to us may be anything but obvious to another person. In considering what that idea might look like from another angle, we can find better ways to explain it or present it. Theory of mind can also help us to remain humble and considerate, by recognizing that our words or actions may be perceived by other people very differently than we intend or expect—for good or for bad. Extroverts may need to learn that a well-intentioned, "Would you like

[9] C. S. Lewis, *An Experiment in Criticism* (Cambridge: Cambridge University Press, 1961), 140–141.

to hear about Jesus?" could be taken as pushy and intrusive; introverts may need to learn that a genuine offer of "Would you like to come to Mass with me?" may in fact be welcomed.

Nor is this humility needed only for people whom we recognize as obviously different from ourselves. As Tolkien points out, it is familiar faces that are "most difficult really to see with fresh attention, perceiving their likeness and unlikeness: that they are faces, and yet unique faces. . . . We say we know them. They have become like the things which once attracted us by their glitter, or their colour, or their shape, and we laid hands on them, and then locked them in our hoard, acquired them, and acquiring ceased to look at them."[10]

What is true of familiar faces can also be true of familiar experiences; theory of mind can help us gain fresh insight into *ourselves* by seeing with another's eyes. When I was newly a Christian, and going through a difficult time in my life, the poetry of Gerard Manley Hopkins was of inestimable value to me. Entering his perspective, one of far more spiritual maturity than mine, showed me that it was possible to respond to the experience of depression in a way that is rooted in deep faith in God. Poems such as "Carrion Comfort" taught me, in a real sense, how to pray, because they allowed me to see what it is *like* to lift up one's suffering to God, in both pain and hope, such that, in the end, I could say in gratitude, with Hopkins,

---

[10] J. R. R. Tolkien, "On Fairy-stories," in *Tolkien On Fairy-stories: Expanded edition, with commentary and notes*, ed. Verlyn Flieger and Douglas A. Anderson (London: HarperCollins, 2014), 67.

"That night, that year / Of now done darkness I wretch lay wrestling with (my God!) my God."

ON DAILY MASS

Sunlight gilds the pine boughs at my window,
Each needle haloed, dark against the light,
As if this evanescent brightness shows
The good this day may hold. The time is tight,
To catch my breath before the press of all
I have to do; the minutes slip away,
The fading sunlight moves along the wall
And I have done so little yet this day.
But still I turn aside, set down my pen,
And heed the deeper call that bids me here.
Agnus Dei, dona nobis pacem.
Time out of time: eternity comes near,
And in the hour I thought I could not spare,
I kneel, and, halting, ask the saints for prayer.

CHAPTER SEVEN

Pain and Doubt

"How can a good and loving God exist when there is such evil in the world?" "Why do innocent people suffer?" "Why has this terrible thing happened to me?" Questions like these have always mattered, and people have always asked them—consider the Book of Job—and we must be ready to address them. Pain and doubt, suffering and evil: these are part of the human experience. Difficult as these topics are, we cannot afford to ignore them; these issues are cited, over and over again, as the causes of crises of faith.

We can begin, paradoxically, by turning the 'problem of evil' on its head. The very fact that we protest evil means that we recognize the reality and ultimate priority of goodness.

Why, after all, is suffering a problem? We recognize that there is something fundamentally *wrong* about certain kinds of events that happen to us, which in turn suggests that we have a deep-seated sense of what the right state of affairs is (even if we have never fully experienced it). We do not take suffering simply as a given, as it would have to be taken if, in reality, the material world is all that there is. Recognition that evil is evil points toward the existence of a moral law. Nearly everyone, if asked, will assert that *some* particular heinous act is wrong (child abuse or racism, for instance), even if they then try to frame their moral response in relativistic or utilitarian terms.

Protesting evil and ugliness means that we instinctively recognize goodness and beauty, and we prefer them—even when the evil, ugly condition is pervasive and persistent. The utter predictability and inevitability of death and disease has not led people to accept them; quite the contrary. A diagnosis of cancer in a friend or loved one alarms and dismays us, no matter how commonplace such an occurrence is. The 'problem of evil' is thus also the 'problem of good': the very fact that we can distinguish good from evil, and that we value the good and reject the evil, suggests the reality of an underlying moral order.

TELLING THE TRUTH

Paradoxically, one of the reasons that pain and suffering are such major issues for apologetics today is that modern Christians have often shied away from dealing with them. It is certainly more pleasant to focus on the joyful aspects of Christianity, but we cannot get to the Resurrection without the Cross. Christian joy is real, but it is not the whole picture. A Christian apologist or writer can create a false narrative, not through bad intentions, but by expressing platitudes, sugar-coating the issues, or wrapping up complex issues too neatly. When a skeptic or a doubting Christian rejects (rightly) the oversimplification, the risk is that they will reject the whole truth along with it. Christians can indeed point toward the evidence of miraculous healings as evidence that God acts in powerful ways, but if we claim that God will immediately heal *every* injury or illness, we are setting people up for a crisis of doubt and a rejection of the Faith if they pray and are not healed. Would we be so quick to utter platitudes like "God won't give you more than you can handle" if we admitted that we might be called to handle martyrdom?

Scripture certainly doesn't hesitate to acknowledge suffering and even to express it at length and with great eloquence: consider the Psalms, Lamentations, Job, and Ecclesiastes. Christians in the medieval through early modern eras were much more comfortable with the facts of death, as it were: consider the *memento mori*, death's-head images intended to remind people that they must face their own demise. But as our technological and medical prowess has grown, so too has grown a tendency to avoid facing the inevitable reality of mortality and suffering.

We live in a fallen world and we are constantly faced with the evidence of our fallen condition. Indeed one of the most profound arguments for the truth of the Christian story is that we have an explanation of why the world is both beautiful and broken, and why we can have moments of joy as well as experiences of tragedy. No other worldview can satisfactorily account for both of those elements. If we want to present the Gospel in a meaningful way, we need to acknowledge the brokenness of the world. If all we present is the happy ending, without recognizing the disruption that brought about the need for the happy ending, we've got nothing of value to say. Here we see the particular role that imaginative apologetics can play through the arts.

Doctrine clarifies what is and is not sin: we need the refreshing, bracing (and challenging) structure of the Church's teaching to avoid getting lost in our own self-doubts or misled by our own self-will. But we cannot convince people of their condition merely by saying, "such-and-such is a sin." The word has lost its meaning in the wider culture (and indeed too often within the Church as well). However, we can help people begin to recognize the meaning of 'sin' and 'evil' from the examples they see before them—the situations and problems that are already distressing and hurting them.

In order to tell the truth, we have to be willing to face darkness, pain, sin, and struggle, and not look away. The Gospel is a *redemption story*. It is a story of God sending his only-begotten Son on a rescue mission to save us. We were in rebellion, and his Son was crucified for us. We must recognize our need to be rescued in order to appreciate that this is the story of a rescue.

We can't really convey this great truth if we just stand on the outside and say Happy Jesus Things. We need to tell stories that show our need for rescue and redemption, and that there is no place so low, no state of weakness too profound, no state of desperation so deep that God cannot find us and rescue us. We have to be willing to go into the darkness and meet people there and say that our God is a crucified God. He is risen and bears the marks of the nails in his hands and feet.

THE EMOTIONAL CONTEXT

When someone brings up the problem of evil, or the problem of suffering, our first priority should be to recognize the reality of the problem and *mourn with those who mourn*. Only in the context of compassion will our arguments have real meaning. Next, if possible, we should determine what kind of question the person has. Is this an intellectual doubt, prompted by the question of suffering in general, or by anti-Christian arguments that he has heard? Or—as is often the case—is the intellectual question coming from an immediate experience with suffering?

If an injustice, a terrible crime, or a personal loss has occurred, our first response should be to express sympathy, to offer help, and to comfort the afflicted. There will be time enough later to consider what it all means. The person whose mother has died, whose child has been diagnosed with leukemia, whose friend or neighbor has been shot, whose hometown has been obliterated by a hurricane, does not need *at that moment* to hear philosophical arguments about evil, however true and useful they are. This person needs, first of all, to be loved, and to know that they can unite their suffering with that of Our Lord Jesus Christ on the Cross, who is with them in their pain; they need to be prayed for, and to be encouraged to pray, for themselves and for those whom they love. First things first.

Recognizing the emotional context of questions is also helpful in determining an appropriate response. The exclamation "I can't possibly believe in God after this has happened!" should not be taken as a sober-minded assessment of a person's philosophical and theological convictions. Rather, it may very well be a cry of frustration and anger, like someone saying, "I hate my job!" after a particularly stressful work-week. Address the feeling, not the statement, at this time, and above all, don't contradict. You may be entirely certain that your friend still believes in God—in fact, you may be correct in that conviction—but it will do no good, and much harm, to say, "No, I'm sure you really *do* believe in God." That's going to sound like a negation of the person's experiences—a denial of their pain—and will, if anything, only encourage that person to affirm more deliberately what was originally just a cry of anguish.

In quieter times, when the crisis has passed and we can talk about the issues, it's important to know how to consider *doubt*. Even the very act of asking a question about the Faith is significant, especially for a Christian, because all too often, Christians are terrified of asking questions. They fear that having doubts means that their faith is in danger, and they fear that having questions will lead to them being condemned as sinful and weak. Unfortunately, these fears are often justified, and those who ask questions are told to "just have faith" or are criticized or rejected for "causing trouble." Unfortunately, this creates the perfect situation for driving people out of the Church: they have questions and can't get them answered; they try to suppress the questions, but the inner tension itself creates more of a problem, and magnifies the significance of the questions. This vicious circle, not the initial questions, is corrosive to their faith. When pastors, ministry leaders, and fellow parishioners feel threatened by doubts and questions, things can go badly wrong. (And this is precisely why we need apologists in the Church!)

ADDRESSING DOUBT

Honest doubt is not to be feared: it is different from the self-seeking, self-serving skepticism that doesn't want to believe because it's more convenient not to. Doubt is part of the human condition; after all, even the disciples, who had been around Jesus for three years, still asked him to *increase their faith*. If they already had perfect faith, they wouldn't have needed to ask him to increase it. Or then you have the wonderful prayer of the man whose son is suffering from fits. He says, 'Lord, I believe! Help my unbelief.' And Jesus heals his son.

How do we help people move from doubt to faith? To begin with, we must distinguish between *doubts*, as in unanswered and troubling questions, and *doubt*, as a state of mind that involves ongoing uncertainty about commitment to the Faith.

As surprising as it may sound, doubts in the first sense (i.e., questions) are good in themselves because they indicate a desire to grow in knowledge and understanding. If our Faith is true, then we need not fear any question! This kind of doubt, if handled rightly, will lead to finding answers and thus, we hope, to a stronger faith.

Doubt as a state of mind is more complex. Sometimes this state of uncertainty comes from the recognition of multiple challenges to one's beliefs, or the realization that competing ideas are more compelling than one initially thought. Sometimes doubt may result from unsettling changes in one's life, such as the transition from living at home to going away to college, or the transition from singlehood to marriage and family. It's natural for major changes to be unsettling; the question is what the person does about this state of mind. If the person recognizes this state of doubt and moves to resolve it, then this is all perfectly healthy and, indeed, is very likely to result in a stronger faith—assuming that there are people who are willing and able to answer the questions.

However, there is a certain kind of doubt that is a condition of the will, not of the intellect. It is possible to have received adequate information and explanations, but still cling to one's own uncertainty. Sometimes this reluctance to accept that one's questions have been answered is a defense against having to move forward and act on one's convictions; sometimes it's an excuse to do what one knows is wrong. Other times, though, it's the result of a misunderstanding about the nature of genuine faith: having the mistaken idea that one must *feel* certain about something in order truly to believe it. A person may well be stuck in a state of doubt because he lacks that feeling of certainty. This is a particularly sticky trap, psychologically, for a number of reasons. For one thing, it makes the person vulnerable to second-guessing his own reactions; if he *wants* to feel certain, he may well mistrust his feeling of certainty, if it arrives, as being generated by wish-fulfillment. For another, a too-close or too-persistent analysis of one's emotional state often has a distorting effect on one's own mental state. But most importantly, the idea that subjective certainty is required for faith is a false expectation to begin with.

Since we are finite creatures, we can never know everything or understand everything completely; there must always be some uncertainty in our life, and yet we act anyway. We trust our friends; we make plans for the future; we make all sorts of decisions in entirely reasonable *confidence* without having *certainty*. We even make plenty of life-changing decisions without either certainty or confidence, but simply with a reasoned judgment that it's the best course. Matters of faith are no different from any other decision. We can't know with 100 percent certitude that a particular job offer is the best one to take, or that it is wise to marry a specific person; we can only make a judgment and act on it. Not to act is also to make a decision. A desire for a false, mathematical certainty about questions of faith is a stumbling block to many who are otherwise convinced; they need to be shown that at this point, faith is a question of the will, not of the intellect.

Doubt can also become something to be indulged in, especially in this modern day when clarity and certainty in matters of religion are looked down upon as bigoted or narrow-minded. Refusing to seek clarity, or refusing to accept truth and move on, is not the same as honest uncertainty; it is a moral issue. If someone refused to ever check his bank balance, preferring the excitement of not knowing whether or not any particular debit-card transaction would be approved or denied, we would not call him open-minded; rather, we would call him irresponsible.

There are several points that we must note, lest we take a simplistic approach to addressing doubts. The first is that we must be willing to acknowledge differences among Christians on certain issues, both in doctrine and in practice, and to give reasons why we believe our Church's position to be correct, without being demeaning or dismissive of the views with which we disagree. In this regard, it is very helpful indeed to know whether the issue is left up to the individual conscience or not. For instance, the question "How old is the Earth?" is a highly divisive one among Christians in America. Catholic teaching, however, does not provide an answer to that question. Catholics are free to follow the evidence and arguments to either a young-earth or an old-earth conclusion, as long as that conclusion includes recognizing that God is the Creator, regardless of how we interpret the timeline of Genesis. If we can admit that "not all Christians agree on such-and-such issue," it gives us more credibility when we make broader statements about the fundamental claims of Christianity, such as the Resurrection or the Trinity.

The second point is that we must not be afraid to say, "I don't know." Paradoxically, we gain credibility as apologists when we are willing to admit the boundaries of our knowledge or understanding. If we try to set ourselves up as having all the answers, it's certain that we'll be winging it on a few of those answers, at least . . . and perhaps even giving inaccurate or misleading responses. To say, "That's a good question; I don't know the answer," also gives the listener more confidence in the answers that you do provide.

When we are faced with a question to which we don't know the answer, we must discern whether or not it's worthwhile to follow up on it. Is the question intended seriously, or is it a rabbit-trail or a distraction (conscious or unconscious)? If it's a serious and relevant question, and you don't know the answer, then it's important to help with the follow-up. Suggest some resources where the questioner can find the answers he is looking for, or promise to follow up yourself (and then do it!). However, if you think that the question is a distraction, it's okay to say, "I don't know, but in any case, it's taking us away from a more significant question, which is such-and-such."

The third point to consider in addressing doubt is

that we should remember that the answers to particular questions may be difficult for an individual person to accept: they may conflict with other beliefs or desires, or they may be too hard to take just at that moment. As faithful Christians, we must neither bully people to come to a conclusion before they are capable of it, nor give in to the temptation to make things easier in the short term by watering down what we believe, whether it's doctrine or ethics. We believe in the bodily resurrection of Our Lord Jesus Christ; this may be hard for a 'spiritual but not religious' person to accept, but it does that person no favors to suggest that he could interpret 'resurrection' in purely spiritual terms. That's simply not true; Our Lord rose bodily. It's better for a skeptic to face that strange claim squarely, than to be offered a falsification of it.

Likewise, we know that God hears all prayers and answers them in the way that is best for our eternal welfare—but his answers may not be what we expect or indeed want at that moment. Especially when it comes to suffering and illness, it can be very hard to understand why God does not seem to be answering our prayers for help and healing, especially when we know that others have been miraculously healed. We must admit that this is difficult, not paper over it. The person who is diagnosed with cancer, or the couple who are unable to have children despite a great longing for children, should indeed pray, and we should pray for them and with them, but we should not promise that God *will* heal or that he *will* cause the couple to conceive. Nor should we in any way suggest that they just need to "pray harder" or "have more faith": that is a terrible cruelty to a suffering person, and is likely to drive them away from God when they need him most. Rather, we should help them first of all to know that God loves them and is with them even in their deepest pain; and then to encourage them to see that suffering can be redemptive, and that they can 'offer it up' to Our Lord on their own behalf and that of others.[1]

HONESTY

If we tell the truth about the experience of pain, our witness is more credible when we speak about joy. When there are Christians who can speak honestly about suffering in their art, it provides the necessary context for other Christians to speak about hope and love. Here, imaginative apologetics can shine, as literature and the arts provide ways to illuminate questions of suffering and joy in ways that argument cannot.

J. R. R. Tolkien's great novel *The Lord of the Rings*—which is, I would argue, the greatest novel of the twentieth century—is one example of what this looks like. In my memoir I write:

> Imaginatively, Tolkien's Middle-earth always felt right; it had the ordinary pleasures and disappointments of life as well as the high excitements and fears. It had a place for both hope and disappointment, achievement and failure. Like the world I lived in, Middle-earth had greater depths than I could take in at any given moment. It was a world in which there is darkness, but also real

[1] See Colossians 1:24.

light, a light that shines in the darkness and is not extinguished: Galadriel's light, and the light of the star that Sam sees break through the clouds in Mordor, and the ray of sun that falls on the flower-crowned head of the king's broken statue at the crossroads.[2]

Perhaps counter-intuitively, if we shy away from sharing any representations of pain, suffering, loss, fear, doubt, and anger, we undercut our own ability to share the truth with people, but if we are honest about these difficult issues, we increase our credibility when we do speak about joy, love, and the peace that passes all understanding.[3]

Let me show you two more examples.

The first is a poem by Gerard Manley Hopkins. A devout Catholic, he suffered from illness and depression throughout his life. He wrote both joyful and extraordinarily dark poems, but even while he's voicing suffering, despair, and frustration, he's always turning to God with a raw honesty that is tremendously refreshing. Hopkins's poetry was helpful in my own coming to faith, and certainly in my growth as a Christian. Here is his lament about his apparent failures as a preacher, teacher, and poet:

"Thou Art Indeed Just, Lord"

Thou art indeed just, Lord, if I contend
With thee; but, sir, so what I plead is just.

---

[2] Holly Ordway, *Not God's Type: An Atheist Academic Lays Down Her Arms* (San Francisco: Ignatius Press, 2014), 25.

[3] Philippians 4:7.

Why do sinners' ways prosper? and why must
Disappointment all I endeavour end?
Wert thou my enemy, O thou my friend,
How wouldst thou worse, I wonder, than thou
 dost
Defeat, thwart me? Oh, the sots and thralls of
 lust
Do in spare hours more thrive than I that spend,
Sir, life upon thy cause. See, banks and brakes
Now, leavèd how thick! lacèd they are again
With fretty chervil, look, and fresh wind shakes
Them; birds build—but not I build; no, but
 strain,
Time's eunuch, and not breed one work that
 wakes.
Mine, O thou lord of life, send my roots rain.

Hopkins is forthright about his frustration. Why, indeed, do sinners' ways prosper? Surely we have all had
that question at some time or another! Hopkins observes
how those who are enslaved to sin, the "sots and thralls of
lust," are thriving, while he, who is faithful, finds himself
a failure. Even the world of nature stands in stark contrast
to his life: bushes grow thick and green, and birds build
their nests, but despite all his effort, his work seems ster-
ile. (Hopkins's poetry only began to be published, and its
merit recognized, after his death.) This poem does not
end with any attempt to fake contentment or comprehension, but rather with his plea to God for something to
alleviate his dry and defeated condition: "Mine, O thou
lord of life, send my roots rain." In this way, he shows

what it looks like to trust in God in the midst of suffering and apparent failure.

Another example is by a contemporary writer, the Anglican poet Malcolm Guite:

"O Clavis"[4]

Even in the darkness where I sit
And huddle in the midst of misery
I can remember freedom, but forget
That every lock must answer to a key,
That each dark clasp, sharp and intricate,
Must find a counter-clasp and meet its guard,
Particular, exact, and intimate,
The clutch and catch that meshes with its ward,
I cry out for the key I threw away
That turned and overturned with certain touch
And with the lovely lifting of a latch
Opened my darkness to the light of day.
O come again, come quickly, set me free
Cut to the quick to fit, the master key.

Here we see the experience of depression—especially its sense of isolation and helplessness—articulated in a way that fits into the Christian experience. Significantly, like Hopkins in "Thou Art Indeed Just, Lord," Guite does not move to resolution within the poem. The speaker remains in darkness, hoping for light but not yet receiving it. Here, we can see that Guite knows how to minister to

---

[4] Malcolm Guite, *Sounding the Seasons: Seventy Sonnets for the Christian Year* (London: Canterbury Press, 2012), 10.

his readers with genuine sympathy and assistance. People who have never experienced depression often do not know how to comfort those who do. With all good intentions, they say things like "cheer up," or "it's not so bad," or offer suggestions on what to do, not recognizing that part of the agony of depression is that it saps one's ability to do *anything*, and that depression is not like an ordinary mood; it does not respond to the will. Trying to cheer up, and inevitably failing, just makes things worse. The poet cries out in prayer: "O come again, come quickly, set me free." Here we see is a deeply Christian response to the reality of the situation, in which the poet recognizes his own weakness and imprisonment, and calls on Christ as the "master key," the only one who can help—and the one who surely will. "O Clavis" provides both compassion and hope, as Guite shows us that even the mental and spiritual suffering of depression is not something to fear, but something to 'offer up' to God. It is a witness to the healing work of Christ.

EUCATASTROPHE

We must recognize the reality of darkness and suffering, and the difficulties that surround faith in our culture today. If we do not, then our presentation of the Faith will likely come across either as coldly intellectual or sentimentally pious—neither of which is particularly appealing. But this is not the whole story: the Catholic faith is the fullness of the truth, and the truth is that our story has a happy ending. There is an important place for a vision of the fallenness of the world, but we also need to help people imaginatively engage with the possibility of *joy*.

As apologists, we can answer questions and present arguments and ideas very convincingly, but we will only have a real impact if people are interested in what we have to say and find it meaningful. Part of our work as imaginative apologists, then, involves stirring up the longing for meaning, truth, beauty, and goodness. We must, in a sense, be gadflies for beauty: rousing people from their contentment with the status quo. As Lewis wrote in "The Weight of Glory," our problem is not that we desire too much, but that we desire too little:

> Indeed, if we consider the unblushing promises of reward and the staggering nature of the rewards promised in the Gospels, it would seem that Our Lord finds our desires not too strong, but too weak. We are half-hearted creatures, fooling about with drink and sex and ambition when infinite joy is offered us, like an ignorant child who wants to go on making mud pies in a slum because he cannot imagine what is meant by the offer of a holiday at the sea. We are far too easily pleased.[5]

What was true in wartime Britain is even more true now, with all the myriad distractions of the Internet age. Christian apologists need to awaken that longing from its slumber, to awaken people from the numbness of over-stimulation and distraction. Literature, the arts, and architecture will serve us well here, helping to show the beauty of

---

[5] C. S. Lewis, "The Weight of Glory," in *The Weight of Glory: And Other Addresses* (San Francisco: Harper, 1949), 26.

Christ, to give a glimpse into the Kingdom: just a glimpse, but enough perhaps to waken curiosity, or a longing for that peace that passes all understanding. For although the Christian story leads through darkness, it leads to joy: "Joy beyond the walls of the world, poignant as grief,"[6] as Tolkien put it, joy that is deeper than mere pleasure or momentary contentment, and that endures as no happiness in our earthly lives can endure.

GRANDMOTHER'S HOUSE

Three hundred years and more this house has stood
Along the gravelled road to Heald Pond,
Its lawns and gardens neighbored by the woods.
I knew it well. But decades now have gone
And I have not returned. Till now. It seems
To be an empty shell, a skeleton
Just like the trees beside: three mighty elms
Struck by disease, but strangely, not cut down;
Limb-lopped in years long past, left to decay.
In childhood I did not find them grim;
They simply *were*, these sentinels in gray,
Who gave no warning as the rot set in . . .
I turn away. I am a stranger here;
The past is gone, is lost, just as I feared.

---

[6] J. R. R. Tolkien, "On Fairy-stories," 75.

CHAPTER EIGHT

Longing

In the previous chapter, we considered the problem of suffering and noted that we recognize evil precisely because we have a deep underlying sense of what *goodness* is. No matter how pervasive or inescapable suffering is, we somehow recognize that it does not, or should not, have the last word. This 'problem of good' opens up the possibility of our intuitions and desires pointing us toward the truth. The value of building on our deep-seated *longing* for the good and the beautiful is so great that it is worth taking the time to develop a well-rounded imaginative apologetics approach to it.

We do not merely *prefer* what is good, beautiful, and meaningful if we can get it. We deeply desire and are always restlessly searching for it, even if we aren't quite sure exactly what we seek or where we can find it. Although it is possible (and unfortunately all too common) to have one's longings for goodness, beauty, and meaning dulled and misdirected, it is part of our common human nature to experience longing for something more than what we experience in the here-and-now. C. S. Lewis called it

Sehnsucht and observed that it could not be identified with any particular experience or pleasure, but was something beyond all of those. This longing can be felt in personal terms—as a desire for meaning and beauty in one's own life—and also as a profound desire for justice, peace, reconciliation, and love in one's society, over against the daily injustices, conflict, hatred, and instability that we see in the news and in our own families and neighborhoods.

We long for love, for connection, for meaning in our lives, and yet complete fulfillment is always just out of reach. Lewis argues that this deep-seated, unfulfilled (and unfulfillable in this world) longing is an indication that we are not merely material creatures:

> Creatures are not born with desires unless satisfaction for those desires exists. A baby feels hunger: well, there is such a thing as food. A duckling wants to swim: well, there is such a thing as water. Men feel sexual desire: well, there is such a thing as sex. If I find in myself a desire which no experience in this world can satisfy, the most probable explanation is that I was made for another world. If none of my earthly pleasures satisfy it, that does not prove that the universe is a fraud. Probably earthly pleasures were never meant to satisfy it, but only to arouse it, to suggest the real thing.[1]

Longing has an important place in imaginative apologetics, both because of its very existence, which challenges

---

[1] Lewis, *Mere Christianity*, 136–137.

the naturalistic paradigm, and because we can point toward God who is the fulfillment of that longing.

Here, however, we must be careful to be precise. The 'argument from desire' is often oversimplified and, in the process, made much less compelling. Just because we *desire* meaning, eternal life, and total fulfillment does not prove either that these things exist or that we will get them—as any thoughtful skeptic will point out—but it does suggest the *possibility* of these things existing and being accessible to us. The fact of a man's hunger does not mean he has bread: he may starve to death. However, the fact that his hunger is capable of being satisfied by bread indicates that food exists somewhere, even if he has none.

Many people recognize the logic of Lewis's point, but are still troubled by the possibility that Christian faith is nothing but wish-fulfillment. If following our desires leads us to faith, then are we simply tricking ourselves into faith because we like it and want it to be true? Here we should pause and consider the nature of this challenge to faith; many atheists find this is a serious question, as indeed it should be.

One form of this skeptical argument against Christianity is that faith is purely psychological in origin: that those who say that they are intellectually convinced are actually self-deluded—they don't *really* think it's true, but are just finding reasons to prop up a belief that makes them feel good. This sort of argument falls apart fairly quickly because it presumes that the questioner knows better than the person himself what he believes. Apologists should take care not to make the same mistake in our own arguments! If an atheist says, "I am contented and experience no existential longing whatsoever," we must not contradict him and say, "Oh yes, you do!" For even though we know that his soul *does* yearn toward God, it is entirely possible that he does not *feel* that yearning or does not recognize it for what it is. To claim that we know his inner life better than he does is arrogant and off-putting. Far better to invite our skeptic to consider whether there might be more to reality than he's even aware of, to suggest that if there is the possibility of even greater joy (indeed, of eternal joy) it's a reasonable thing to find out if it might be true.

A second skeptical counter-argument is to say that the Christian hope for heaven is mere pie in the sky, a pleasing tale made up to distract us from the misery of our lives and keep us in our places: that it is the 'opiate of the masses.' It's not actually true, merely useful to the ruling classes, the atheist will argue. One good response to this claim is to point out that historically, it is simply not the case. Christian witness through the ages shows that those who are most convinced that their deepest desires are fulfilled in God are precisely those who sacrifice life, health, safety, reputation, time, money, and comfort to help others: serving the poor, caring for the sick, teaching the ignorant, counseling the doubtful and overburdened, challenging oppressors, working tirelessly for the benefit of others. The lives of the saints—ancient, medieval, modern—are an important part of our overall apologetics argument.

However, both personal witness and the witness of the saints are, unfortunately, likely to hit that same brick wall: "You think it's true because you just *want* it to be true."

(Case, apparently, closed.) This challenge to Christian hope is devilishly difficult to address, because ultimately it's not really an argument at all, but rather an assumption: that reality is finally unsatisfying, bleak, and disappointing. We will explore this issue in more detail.

THE FACT OF LONGING

At the outset, it's important to distinguish between the *fact* of human longing and the specifics of what we long *for*. Most skeptics present the wish-fulfillment claim as a response to the latter issue, but ignore the former entirely—but it is the former issue that has the deepest significance. The question that disrupts the materialist paradigm is this: *why* do we desire meaning in our lives?

Why do people so often feel a desire for something more—something they can't even articulate, perhaps— even when they are fed, clothed, sheltered, and entertained?

A common materialist response is to say that we are wired by evolution to seek out more than we have, and that this incessant search benefits either individuals or the human race by ensuring that we have a surplus of what we need, or that we are always discovering new resources. It may indeed be the case that spiritual restlessness brings about some useful material results, but it is more reasonably understood as a side effect, not as a cause, of our longing. (Many writers find ways to procrastinate in plausibly useful ways when a book or article deadline approaches—doing laundry, tidying up one's desk, answering emails, and so on—but we would be mistaken to say that writers accept book projects as a motivation to do housework.)

Just because the evolutionary paradigm can offer an answer doesn't, in itself, mean that it's the correct answer. Our sense of longing often involves dissatisfaction with the accumulation of material things and rejection of a state of superficial contentment; it does not seem to be satisfied the way that hunger or tiredness can be satisfied by a meal or a good night's sleep. Desires for food and sleep recur, of course, but each individual occurrence of the desire *can* be fully satisfied.

In contrast, the human desire for meaning and joy is never fully satisfied (only distracted or dulled) by *material* things. It suggests that this desire for meaning at least points toward the reality and significance of a non-material dimension to the world. As humans, we seem to need both material things (food, shelter, clothing) and non-material things (love, connection, purpose).

We can make the case, then, that human beings have a deep-seated desire for something more than the material world affords. So far, so good: but this is not itself an argument for the truth of the Faith. Our desires can be at least partially satisfied in our earthly lives by non-material goods: for instance, by the experience of loving and being loved, by spiritual experiences in the context of other religions or belief systems, or by profound aesthetic experiences in literature, art, music, or nature. These are all contexts in which someone can have a genuine experience of the transcendent, and one that (at least for the time being) is satisfying.

Where, then, does the Christian claim enter the picture? Our sense of longing and inability to be fully satisfied suggests the *possibility* of a transcendent good for which we were made, but we must still use our reason to determine whether or not the possibility is true.

SKEPTICISM AND PESSIMISM

Our modern culture is paradoxically both extremely suggestible (hence the success of advertising) and extremely wary of being taken in. The Christian claim is often resisted precisely *because* it is appealing: the more attractive our picture of the Faith is, the more likely it will seem to some people that we have simply made it up, imagining exactly those things that will most appeal to us. The better it sounds, in short, the less likely it is to be true. This pessimistic view is strangely compelling: some skeptics present this line of argument triumphantly, in mockery of Christians, but others do so regretfully, convinced that their desire to embrace the Faith is, paradoxically, the very reason that they must refuse to do so.

True, it is irrational to conclude that because we want something, it *must* exist—but it is equally irrational to believe that because we want something, it *cannot* exist. A man lost in the desert sees an oasis in the distance: is it a mirage, or the real thing? It could be either one; the only rational thing to do is to go find out. It would be madness to ignore the possibility of the oasis and keep trekking across barren sands to die of thirst just because that glimpse of hope *might* be a hallucination. C. S. Lewis gives us a fictional treatment of this with the dwarves in *The Last Battle*, who are so afraid of being 'taken in' by Aslan that they are ultimately incapable of being 'taken out' of their self-imposed prison.

We can be so afraid of tricking ourselves by wishful

thinking that we deceive ourselves by fearful thinking. An unemployed person looks at a job advertisement that is perfectly suited for his skills and interests: it would be equally foolish to behave as if he's absolutely sure to get the job, and thus not even to prepare for the interview, and to behave as if he had no chance whatsoever, and thus not even bother to apply. In short, whether we want something or not, whether it is a supremely desirable thing or not, has no direct bearing on the question "Is it true?" It only tells us that the thing is possible.

Certainly, many different religions and ethical systems (including atheism) make promises, and as those promises contradict each other, the promises cannot all be entirely true. In fact, most of them are false, to a greater or lesser degree. This is, in fact, just what we might expect if there is such a thing as the truth, and one way to the truth. If this truth is only half-glimpsed, guessed at, or partially understood, then naturally it will be folded into systems other than that of the Christian faith, and wrapped up with a great deal that isn't true. Furthermore, those who wish to deceive can borrow language and images from the true way in order to profit by making their own option more attractive.

The pessimist can always find reasons to be suspicious. Perhaps the job listing is out of date; the job may well be filled already. Perhaps some of the listings are scams, intended to get names and personal details so as to hack into people's bank accounts. Perhaps some of the ads are not really for jobs at all, but are part of a sociological study on the effect of certain rhetorical choices in job-ad language on application rates. Perhaps it is a front for snatching victims for slavery and sexual trafficking. Sadly, these things do happen. But it would be very foolish to then conclude that it's not worth applying for any jobs at all.

Because so many people are so fearful of being taken in, we must be careful not to be pushy or to paint an over-rosy picture when we suggest that they look into the Faith. We can invite them, and suggest that they may want to take a look, but we should not promise that they will be immediately convinced or transformed. We can recognize the reality of pain, death, injustice, and sorrow, and mourn with those who mourn. And we can remind them that the Faith is not easy: we are, after all, following a crucified Lord, who calls his followers to take up their own crosses.

CULTIVATING LONGING

So far we have been talking about following up on a sense of longing, taking for granted that we all feel it. However, our culture is one that works to deaden our desire for the transcendent and to divert what remains into materialistic and sensual channels: usually shopping and sex. People do feel a yearning for the good, the true, and the beautiful, but this yearning is often stunted and weak, like seedlings sprouting in the dark.

How, then, do we help to cultivate this 'holy longing' in ways that will bear fruit?

One way is through stories that evoke joy and make our Christian joy *credible*. As we have seen, we must recognize the reality of pain and suffering in the world; otherwise we lack all credibility. We have hope, but our faith is not a get-out-of-suffering-free card. However, although we don't want to present a simplistic, sentimental picture that denies the brokenness of the world, we must also re-sist the tendency to swing too far the other way. In recent years, secular literature and art, and particularly film and television, has shown a tendency to dwell on the negative (anti-heroes, violence, bleakness), presenting a bleak, even dystopian vision of reality, and certainly one without a firm moral foundation.

What we need are convincing portraits of Christian hope and joy. These are hard to find, but they do exist, and we can find them in some of the most enduring and beloved Christian literature of the twentieth Century: Tolkien's *The Lord of the Rings* and Lewis's Chronicles of Narnia. Both Tolkien and Lewis are forthright about pain and suffering: consider Frodo and Sam's agonizing journey on foot to Mount Doom, or the fact that Lewis shows the destruction of Narnia and the death of a whole host of beloved characters in *The Last Battle*. In turn, both Tolkien and Lewis are able to present a compelling vision of ultimate joy. It's worth noting that neither Tolkien nor Lewis wins over every reader. Some readers of Narnia, for instance, fixate on the apparent exclusion of Susan from the happy ending; some readers of *The Lord of the Rings* simply can't abide the presence of elves. The author must take risks, and no author or artist can connect with ev-ery individual in the audience. However, what we can see, pre-eminently in our two examples here, is a pattern of response. Readers and viewers are moved by the happy ending of a story—above all, one that has come through genuine difficulty or darkness.

Tolkien coined a word to describe this sort of hap-py ending: *eucatastrophe*. It means "the good catastrophe":

the unexpected happy ending, which gives us a profound taste of joy. Tolkien argues that the response we have to a happy ending is in fact a pointer toward the truth of the Gospel: our reaction "may be a far-off gleam or echo of *evangelium* in the real world."[2] We respond to the happy ending of a story with joy because it echoes the story that God himself is creating: the story that began in the Garden and—after darkness and pain—will bring us to the new heaven and the new earth.

All of human history is a story, Tolkien says, and it is one with a happy ending:

> The Birth of Christ is the eucatastrophe of Man's history. The Resurrection is the eucatastrophe of the story of the Incarnation. This story begins and ends in joy. It has pre-eminently the "inner consistency of reality." There is no tale ever told that men would rather find was true, and none which so many sceptical men have accepted as true on its own merits. For the Art of it has the supremely convincing tone of Primary Art, that is, of Creation. To reject it leads either to sadness or to wrath.[3]

If we look at modern literature, art, film, and television—not to mention the news—we will indeed see a great deal of both sadness (often in the form of apathy or depression) and wrath. The best Christian art and liter-

[2] Tolkien, "On Fairy-stories," 77.
[3] Ibid., 78.

ature provides a eucatastrophic vision, one that suggests that these are not the only options: we can have a realistic hope for something more. Tolkien, master fantasist, underscores the point: our joy is not mere wish-fulfillment or escapist dreaming. The Christian story, he says, "is supreme; and it is true. Art has been verified. God is the Lord, of angels, and of men—and of elves. Legend and History have met and fused."[4]

IMAGINATIVE SPACE

Thus far I have focused on narrative art, but imaginative apologetics can operate in a variety of ways, both to evoke longing for truth, goodness, and beauty, and to orient that longing toward its divine source. Music and the visual arts may come readily to mind, but it's worth stretching a bit more and considering an ancient, but often overlooked, form of apologetics: namely, architecture.

The buildings in which we live, work, and worship both reflect what we believe and shape our lives. Architecture has a direct, daily impact: in our routine at home, while out shopping, at work, at the park, we are surrounded and influenced by the shapes of stone, glass, brick, concrete, and wood, the patterns of light and shade, and the decorations (or lack thereof).

The church is particularly important architecturally, as it is far more than an assembly space for a group of Christians; it is the setting for the source and summit of Christian life, the Eucharist; it is where Christ himself meets us. The physical environment for this meeting of

---

[4] Ibid.

heaven and earth speaks volumes about what we believe, and provides the opportunity for communicating this with all who enter.

Traditional church architecture and imagery is a language developed over the centuries of the Church's life, varying in its dialect in different times and places, but with a common grammar of the sacred. The church building represents the ark of salvation; it should suggest to us that we are being drawn into heaven, in the communion of the saints. The tabernacle, holding the Body of Our Lord himself, in a place of honor, reminds us that he is our King. The graceful pillars and arches, the stained glass windows, and the baptismal font and holy water stoups remind us that we are in no ordinary hall. Candles and colored vestments speak their own symbolic language; paintings, statues, and icons of Jesus and Mary, of the saints and angels, of scenes from Scripture, remind us wherever we look that we are part of something far greater than ourselves.

This exuberance and richness of sensory details—from the touch of holy water to the smell of incense to the sound of bells and chanting—is neither accidental nor extraneous to our faith. To be sure, in one sense it is not necessary: Mass can be celebrated in the very plainest and simplest of settings, and in times of persecution must be. But given even a modicum of safety and freedom to worship, Christians have always built beautiful churches and adorned the liturgy with music and color—and the reason is that it draws us closer to the One who is all Beauty, as he is all Truth and Goodness.

God is the Creator, the ultimate artist. Every bit of natural beauty comes from his hand; our own ability to see and respond to beauty comes from being made in his image. Responding to beauty in the here-and-now, the world that God made (and called good), is a foretaste of how we will rejoice in the eternal, dynamic, unfading beauty in the redeemed creation.

Certainly, all the money used to build a church and make it beautiful could be given to the poor instead, but this would be a failure to see the full humanity of those we serve. Yes, we must meet the physical needs of the poor, but we must also help satisfy their hunger for beauty and meaning, nourishing heart and soul as well as body. The affluent and able-bodied often take for granted being able to have beautiful things at home, or having the time, money, and transportation to attend concerts or visit museums. These things are out of reach of many people, but a church with open doors makes sacred beauty available to all, freely. And indeed, it is spiritually significant that a truly beautiful church is built and decorated in ways that are beyond the reach of any individual person, whether rich or middle-class or poor. It can be a fruitful reminder to us all of our own genuine poverty of spirit. We all come to God with empty hands.

Beauty in worship can further orient us toward the divine. To experience beauty that is intentionally oriented toward the living God is a gift that cannot be used up. It is a vision into the very nature of God, who is the source of all that is good. It can open up a window in the heart for the light of Christ to shine into.

A gracefully proportioned church, drawing the eye up to the altar; windows in plain or stained glass, letting sunbeams in; beautiful vestments worn by the priests and deacons, reminding us that we are at no ordinary gathering, but at the Marriage Supper of the Lamb; music, or sacred silence; candles; icons; gold and red and blue, rich colors for our King; beauty in proportion and graceful design even if there is little ornament. All this says, "Here is the place where we have come to meet the Bridegroom."

Architecture, sacred art, sacred music, and divine liturgy are thus profoundly important in shaping Christian belief.[5] Because of this interconnection between belief and environment, the interior and the exterior, the church building, sacred art, and the liturgy all have a role in *communicating* the truth as well as reflecting it.

The fact that the beauty in a church is objective—available for the aesthetic appreciation of the atheist or agnostic as much as for the believer—is part of its value for imaginative apologetics. *We* know to whom the beauty points; the skeptic may not follow us that far (at least not yet) but he can be drawn forward and invited to contemplation. The beauty offered by a church of traditional design (whether old or new in its construction), and the meaningfulness of its design and symbolism, are available for the skeptic to consider without the pressure of argument and decision. It is not necessary for the skeptic to know all the meaning of the symbolism in the church's art and design; some of it becomes apparent in the action of the liturgy, and some of it is, in any case, accessible by intuition; but the very existence of depths of meaning,

---

beyond the surface, is itself a statement about our Faith: that it is living, with more always available to discover; that in it we have discovered Beauty that is ever ancient and ever new.

Architecture, art, music, and literature all have in common, as well, that they invite but do not impose. The skeptic is enabled to take a step inside, literally or figuratively, and to be involved in some way with this beauty. It may well speak to the longings of his heart: saying "Look, here you will find what you seek." Or it may unsettle him, provoke him to questioning and wondering. If we have been able to offer real beauty, the one thing that we can say is that he will not leave the church, or close the book, entirely unchanged.

Literature and the arts have much to offer us in our apologetics work. It is not the same thing as making an argument in the form of a story; rather, at its best, it *shows* the truth and helps us desire it. It is not a substitute for teaching about doctrine, but it helps us see what doctrine *means*, and suggests that we might want to discover whether it is really true.

GRACE

On the Memorial Service to C. S. Lewis,
Poets' Corner, Westminster Abbey, 22 November 2013

Noon-tide on Saint Cecilia's day, and here
In England's royal church, I sit and watch
The winter sunlight streaming in, gold, clear,
Silent, pure, almost solid to the touch.
Nor is it fairy-gold; it does not fade.
For though that glorious beam of autumn light
Sank down to dusk, to darkness, died that day,
In living memory it still shines bright.
Within that golden light, the choir sings—
The notes resound in blood and bone, as if
I breathed the music in like air; it brings
Me to the point of tears, this time-bound gift
So unexpected, undeserved: a grace
To hold with joy through all my dying days.

CHAPTER NINE

LIMITATIONS AND DANGERS

WE have, hitherto, been focusing on the strengths of the imaginative approach to apologetics: the way that imagination can help us to restore meaning to the language that we use, to find fresh ways to communicate the truth, to develop a more incarnational approach to apologetics, to address the problem of pain and suffering, and to build on the innate human longing for beauty as we help people come to Christ. So far, so good. However, there is no silver bullet for apologetics—no single argument and also no single approach. Imaginative apologetics is not and cannot be *the* definitive strategy for the twenty-first century; it needs to be part of a larger, integrated approach to apologetics, evangelization, discipleship, and catechesis for it to bear fruit to its full potential. The imaginative approach must be paired with argument; it cannot stand alone.

Earlier, we saw that the imagination is connected to the divine nature; it is an aspect of our being made in the image of God. Genesis chapter two shows us more of what it means to be made in the image of the Creator. The first specific task that God gives to Adam, after the responsibility to tend the Garden of Eden, is to name the animals: "So out of the ground the Lord God formed every animal of the field and every bird of the air, and brought them to the man to see what he would call them; and whatever the man called every living creature, that was its name."[1] God chooses to give the work of naming the animals to humankind.

Naming is not only a creative act, it is a *free* creative act, which means that Adam and Eve were free to use their creative gift badly. Our first parents chose to rebel against God, and thus we bear the consequences of the Fall. Our imagination, as with every other human faculty, suffers from the stain of original sin, and so it can be, and indeed often is, used against God—just as our intellect, our will, and our emotions can rebel against God.

The imagination can fail us; it can lead us into error. Some Christians have, on that basis, attempted to suppress the exercise of the imagination or the enjoyment of imaginative literature. But the attempt to suppress it is doomed to worse than failure, for if the imagination is neglected or abused, it will not die, but it will be stunted, and may grow twisted, distorting or diminishing the spiritual and mental health of the whole person. As we have seen, the imagination is a fundamental human faculty, necessary for the exercise of reason. We cannot think unless we have things to think about, and it is the imagination (recognized or unrecognized) that brings meaningful images to our intellect.

---

[1] Genesis 2:19.

But the intellect can fail us, as well as the imagination. As Tolkien notes:

> Fantasy can, of course, be carried to excess. It can be ill done. It can be put to evil uses. It may even delude the minds out of which it came. But of what human thing in this fallen world is that not true? Men have conceived not only of elves, but they have imagined gods, and worshipped them, even worshipped those most deformed by their authors' own evil. But they have made false gods out of other materials: their notions, their banners, their monies; even their sciences and their social and economic theories have demanded human sacrifice. *Abusus non tollit usum.*[2]

Both reason and imagination can go wrong—and so it is prudent for apologists to be aware of the potential weak points and problem areas for imaginative apologetics.

AUTHORITY

One of the greatest strengths of the imaginative approach is the use of narrative and imagery, to draw people into an experience, which offers something different from a propositional statement. Literature and the arts, for instance, can provide a glimpse of the world as Christians see it, so that a skeptic can for a moment see the world in the light of Christ. The imaginative approach can help draw in someone who would otherwise never seriously consider

---

[2] Tolkien, "On Fairy-stories," 65–66.

doctrine or philosophy, and it can (as we have seen) 'incarnate' abstract ideas so that a person can more deeply and fully engage with them.

A challenge for imaginative apologetics in the modern era, however, is that people often have difficulty moving to the next step. It is entirely possible, in this culture, that people will find the Christian faith interesting, even meaningful, yet not be interested in the question of whether it is *true*. Or, less noticeably, people may (and often do) accept Christianity only insofar as they, personally, find it to be acceptable: each doctrinal point weighed and possibly rejected. Someone who accepts Christian teaching on the basis that it is beautiful and meaningful has come far, but has not come quite far enough unless he also accepts it as *true*—independent of his own preferences and views, even contrary to his own preferences and views.

Here we encounter a problem. One of the defining characteristics of our time is the emphasis on the individual as sole arbiter of all decisions, practical and moral, and the concomitant rejection of *authority*. We can see the deep-seated rejection of any authority outside the self in the all-too-common cry (even among Christians) of "Who are *you* to tell me what to believe, what to do, what is right or wrong?" But the test of faith is obedience (see Luke 11:28), and obedience becomes most fully visible when it is contrary to one's own inclinations. Eventually, we will encounter a point of doctrine or authoritative teaching that we dislike, or have difficulty accepting, or simply cannot fully understand, whether it be sexual morality or the Trinity or some other 'hard saying'—and then, obedience is needed.

However, the idea of an ultimate Authority is deeply abhorrent to the modern mind—even more so, I dare say, than the principle of original sin. Here, I do not mean simply an ultimate moral authority; it's not necessarily unpalatable to recognize that God, in an abstract sense at least, is the ultimate moral arbiter. I mean something more subtle: that there is an authority for doctrine, and for the content of our faith as it applies to our daily lives, and that this authority does not belong to the individual. The idea of individual, personal judgment as the (hidden) final arbiter for the living out of our moral code is deeply ingrained into modern culture, even among Christians. We are too easily tempted into thinking that "I agree (or disagree) with this doctrine" is the last word on the subject, as if our agreement or disagreement was what *determined* its truth or falsity. Even the language of conversion can be problematic in this regard, as I discovered when I wrote my own spiritual memoir; it is all too easy to describe one's coming to the Faith in egocentric terms. Jesus Christ is Lord of all; this is a fact. My acceptance of him as Lord does not *grant* him any authority that he does not already have, but rather is a recognition on my part of his existing sovereignty.

A certain amount of what we believe can be discerned through Natural Law, as we intuitively recognize certain moral principles,[3] and is thus independently available for any man or woman to realize. However, there are other, es-

---

[3] For an illuminating discussion of objective morality with a great deal of relevance for imaginative apologetics, see C. S. Lewis, *The Abolition of Man: A Critical Edition by Michael Ward*. This is a highly useful edition, with introduction, commentary, and notes (Chicago: Teller Books, 2017).

sential parts of our faith that are truths of revelation. These truths are given to us; we can recognize their reasonableness after the fact, but we would never have been able to discover them or reason our way to them independently. The Trinity is a prime example. So far, so uncontroversial for the Christian at least. But this is precisely the problem for our modern age. Truths of revelation are *given*, not worked out by the individual. They must be accepted as they are, as they are taught by the Church; to pick and choose parts of the revealed truth and reject others is heresy. If one rejects the revealed truth that Jesus is fully God and fully man, begotten and not made, and instead considers Jesus to be a creature, that is the heresy of Arianism, for instance.[4]

It is perfectly reasonable for anyone to ask for an explanation of the Church's teaching, and to want to understand how it all fits together. But in the modern day, too often the individual person relies on his or her own independent judgment about whether to accept any particular teaching, and in making that judgment, does not consider the credibility of the source or the reliability of the source. The very fact that someone offers an alternative view is considered evidence enough not to believe the traditional view.

How do you decide between two competing ideas? If you are cynical, and you believe that everyone has an agenda, or that everything is about the hermeneutics of power, then there is no way to discern rightly. If you distrust

---

[4] Although it took the Church some time fully to understand and articulate truths such as this in precise theological terms, the truth itself is given to us (not invented or decided upon by the Church).

authority *a priori*—not because it's a flawed authority, or a false authority, but simply because it's authority—then there is no way to make a judgment except on personal preference. All that remains is *I like this*; not, *This is true.*

Imaginative approaches alone will not always suffice to bring people to the point of decision. We must offer a meaningful, compelling story, yes. But we must also bring people to realize that they must decide whether they believe the story also to be true.

THE PROBLEMS OF NARRATIVE

Here we can see, then, both the promise and peril of narrative, in particular, for apologetics. If we rely too heavily on simply sharing an experience, however meaningful and beautiful that experience is, we run the risk of competing on the basis of personal stories—a losing game. For every converted atheist we present, the skeptic can drag out a disillusioned ex-Christian. This degenerates very quickly, often into denials of the other's experience ("You were never really an atheist!" or "You were never really a Christian!") or into a sort of Who's Who of converts. It also suggests, misleadingly, that faith is a numbers game. Even if, in the coming years, far more people abandon their faith than come into the Church, this would not affect the reality of the Church or the truth of her teaching in the least.[5] I hope this does not happen, but it might; and in the deepest sense, it is irrelevant.

I am convinced of the value of personal witness—I

---

[5] For a compelling fictional treatment of this topic, see Robert Hugh Benson's apocalyptic novel *The Lord of the World.*

have, after all, written a memoir of my own conversion! But perhaps it is because I have myself written a conversion story that I am more keenly aware that such stories can be misused. The fact that I, myself, have become a Catholic is not in itself particularly relevant; I don't want people to look at me, but rather to look where I am looking, to see the One on whom my gaze rests. A conversion story can correct misunderstandings; it can open up possibilities; it can help the reader recognize the difficulties and distinctive features of another person's life; it can, and should, invite the reader to consider: could this be true? But it cannot *by itself* be convincing.

That's because narrative is not *in itself* an argument—and much of the difficulty of modern apologetics engagement, particularly on sexual ethics and life issues, stems from the confusion between the two. Marc Barnes, in his incisive analysis of this issue, notes that "Whenever a group comes under moral criticism, our political instinct is to present their 'real life stories.' . . . 'Do you actually *know* any transgender/divorced/fascist/vegan couples?'"[6] Once the "real life story" is in front of us, we are deeply hesitant to make any claims that might offend, hurt, or trouble the subject of the story. The principle is everywhere, applied on the small scale as well as the large, among Christians as well as between Christians and non-believers.[7]

---

[6] Marc Barnes, "The Difference Between a Narrative and an Argument, Part 1," <http://www.patheos.com/blogs/badcatholic/2016/06/the-difference-between-a-narrative-and-an-argument.html>.

[7] Recently I saw an article 'arguing' that Catholic children under the age of seven (the age for First Holy Communion) should not be denied communion, because the author's toddler loves Jesus and wants

One problem with narrative-as-argument is that, as Barnes points out, it makes people into objects in the culture wars, and assumes that they 'are' their choices (and cannot choose differently). Under the pretext of respecting a person, for instance "Cindy the Scientologist," the narrative-as-argument approach hinders us from challenging her beliefs at all: "She *is* her life-story—neat, fixed, bow-tied, and only a horrible bigot would question the content of her narrative."[8] An assumption has been smuggled in: in this case, the assumption that religious beliefs are not objectively true, but are mere preferences about which we cannot argue, any more than we would argue about a preference for chocolate over vanilla ice cream.

> From a logical point of view, narrative only amounts to moral argument by sneaking some general principles through the back door. And of course, this is how narrative arguments *actually* function. By "showing" the life of this or that moral or immoral agent, they implicitly endorse or denounce the moral ideal by which he does or does not live.[9]

But because the arguments in narrative are implicit rather than explicit, they remain nearly always unchallenged; the

---

to receive him at the altar. Whatever the merits of lowering the age to receive communion might be, this particular example was not, in fact, an argument at all, but an observation that children find it difficult to wait for what they want.

8 Marc Barnes, "The Difference Between a Narrative and an Argument, Part 2," <http://www.patheos.com/blogs/badcatholic/2016/06/the-difference-between-a-narrative-and-an-argument-part-2.html>.

9 Barnes, Part 1.

audience is expected to accept or reject the narrative as a whole. The result is that anyone trying to draw attention to the underlying moral question is forced into an antagonistic role from the start (and is likely to be accused of overthinking things, if not of outright bigotry).

NARRATIVE IN ITS PROPER PLACE

What, then, is the place of narrative in apologetics? If we cede the narrative ground entirely, and attempt to rely *only* on propositional argument, then we will lose the battle for *meaning* in the wider culture. Consider, for instance, the complete cultural success of normalizing 'gay marriage,' a maneuver which relies, as we saw in an earlier chapter, on changing the meaning of the word 'marriage.' The argument for this cultural shift was seldom made explicitly; rather, narrative-as-hidden-argument was embedded in the mass media: in advertisements, films, television, and Internet memes as much as in news and commentary. We were, and are, immersed in a sea of assumptions, all the more difficult to fight because they never present themselves in their proper form. Human-interest stories on gay couples create the implicit (or now, explicit) argument that the *only* reason to deny marriage to gay people is bigotry. The statement "They love each other!" puts us on the defensive: "Yes, but. . . ." The problem, meanwhile, is that marriage has been redefined. As long as the begetting and bearing of children was central to the definition of marriage, there was no question of whether two men or two women *should* or *should not* marry; it was clear that they *could not* marry, because their union (sinful or not, socially helpful or not) was something other than marriage. Once contraception became the cultural norm, the definition of marriage dissolved; now, in the wider culture, marriage is taken to be little more than "that friendship I currently consider to be the most important in my life." Christians are handicapped in the duel of narratives by our comparative lack of compelling narratives and imagery to convey the beauty and meaningfulness of fidelity, fertility, openness to children, chastity, self-denial, and self-sacrifice.

As we have seen, problems will arise if we attempt to counter false narratives only with other narratives. Narrative cannot stand alone as our only apologetics enterprise. However, it is enormously fruitful as part of an integrated whole. To return once more to Barnes's analysis:

> There is, however, something exciting about the cultural turn to narrative. Generally speaking, we are far better at holding vague moral positions and general rules than believing that these moral insights should determine how we, our children, and our neighbors should act. . . . Narrative, simply by showing an actual person held in judgment by our moral beliefs, brings up the whole difficulty of applying our principles to the real world. . . . Since living a righteous life, as opposed to thinking right thoughts, is arduous, it's usually easier to drop the moral beliefs the moment any narrative makes them *real*.[10]

---

[10] Barnes, Part 2.

Thus, the embodied doctrine of a story can help to convict us of our own weakness, to see the gap between professed and lived beliefs, as well as to give a glimpse of what truth looks like when it is lived out consistently.

Apologists can also learn a great deal from studying the stories produced by those who do not share our faith, not least to develop a sympathetic understanding of their difficulties. One of the most important questions that an apologist can ask is "*Why* does this person have difficulty accepting the Christian faith?" To identify the obstacles and recognize their seriousness is not the same thing as accepting that these obstacles are insuperable. Rather, the experience of entering into that person's narrative can help us to identify how best to help remove those obstacles.[11]

INTEGRATION

Imaginative expression and propositional argument must work together, if our claims are to be both coherent and compelling. Propositional statements about doctrine or philosophy will do little or nothing if people do not find them meaningful and if they are not embodied in some way, in life or art—but equally, narrative or aesthetic presentations need the bones and ligaments of specific ideas, doctrines, and philosophical claims if they are to help people move toward the truth. By itself, an experience is simply an experience. To make sense of it, we must have an interpretive frame to understand the experience—what it

[11] For an excellent example of this process, see Nabeel Qureshi's memoir *Seeking Allah, Finding Jesus: A Devout Muslim Encounters Christianity* (Grand Rapids, MI: Zondervan, 2014), in which he recounts his journey from being a devout follower of Islam to becoming a Christian.

means, how it relates to or conflicts with what we believe.

Theologian Austin Farrer once commented on C. S. Lewis's book *The Problem of Pain*, saying that "We think we are listening to an argument, in fact we are presented with a vision; and it is the vision that carries conviction."[12] I would venture to differ somewhat with Farrer here and suggest that Lewis's great gift as an apologist (and indeed as a writer in general) is that his writing is so thoroughly integrated. Both argument and imagination are present, each drawing strength from the other. In contrast to dry, abstruse philosophical volumes on suffering, *The Problem of Pain* is vividly realized—Lewis does offer a "vision" of the way he understands this issue, and invites us to enter into it. But it "carries conviction" because it is also grounded in clear reasoning—in argument.

In fact, Lewis provides a very useful conceptual model for the way that imagination and reason can interact fruitfully—a model that will serve us well in apologetics.

ENJOYMENT AND CONTEMPLATION

In "Meditation in a Toolshed," C. S. Lewis distinguishes between looking *at* something and looking *along* something. To "look at" something is to apprehend, to grasp something intellectually by reason, and is what Lewis elsewhere calls "Contemplation": it takes the form of an exterior or outside perspective on the thing that is being thought about. To "look along" something is to comprehend, to engage with something experientially by the physical senses or by imagination. The process of engaging in comprehension of

---

[12] Farrer, "The Christian Apologist," in *Light on C. S. Lewis*, 37.

something is what Lewis calls "Enjoyment": it takes the form of an interior, inside perspective, participating in the thing rather than thinking about it.

Our culture tends to privilege the analytical, detached viewpoint over the experiential one, to the point that looking *at* something analytically is often considered to be the only real way of knowing;[13] looking *along* something experientially is dismissed as merely subjective. As a result, influenced by naturalism, skeptics tend to look *at* the Faith as an object of study (and often censure) and seldom *along* it in an attempt to understand it from inside. Lewis saw the early stages of this process: "The people who look at things have had it all their own way; the people who look along things have simply been brow-beaten. It has even come to be taken for granted that the external account of a thing somehow refutes or 'debunks' the account given from inside."[14] In fact some things cannot be understood solely at the analytical level—like falling in love:

> A young man meets a girl. The whole world looks different when he sees her. Her voice reminds him of something he has been trying to remember all his life, and ten minutes casual chat with her is more precious than all the favours that all other women in the world could grant. He is, as they say, 'in love.' Now comes a scientist and describes this

[13] Using a highly circumscribed meaning for 'real' that excludes at least half of reality, that is, the reality of the spiritual world.

[14] C. S. Lewis, "Meditation in a Toolshed," *God in the Dock: Essays on Theology and Ethics*, ed. Walter Hooper (Grand Rapids, MI: William B. Eerdmans, 1970), 213.

young man's experience from the outside. For him it is all an affair of the young man's genes and a recognised biological stimulus. That is the difference between looking *along* the sexual impulse and looking at it.[15]

If we take only the outsider's perspective to look at human life, then it becomes difficult, if not impossible, to identify or articulate concepts of virtue or morality.

Looking at a man's relationship with his wife, his loving behavior toward her can be seen as a psychological way to cultivate closeness that meets his emotional needs. His emotional needs can be looked at in terms of endorphins produced by his brain, leading to pleasurable sensations. If the outside view is the only way of considering the relationship between husband and wife, it is perfectly reasonable to conclude that when the relationship fails to produce the desired level of physical or emotional pleasure, the man (or woman) is justified in seeking a more satisfactory relationship. The man's desire may be to cheat on his wife; why should he not? The significance of this particular case is particularly clear in light of the breakdown in marriage and sexual ethics in American culture.[16] It is difficult to even articulate Christian ideas about marriage, let alone defend them, using only the analytical language of looking *at* things. Such is the situation with many, if not most, Christian ideas and claims in the broader culture.

[15] Ibid., 212.

[16] See works such as Donna Freitas's *Sex and the Soul: Juggling Sexuality, Spirituality, Romance, and Religion on America's College Campuses* (Oxford: Oxford University Press, 2008).

However, it is important to caution against letting the pendulum swing too far in the opposite direction. As Lewis rightly notes, these are two equally valid modes of knowing, and Lewis is clear that both modes are necessary: "One must look both *along* and *at* everything. In particular cases we shall find reason for regarding one or the other vision as inferior . . . we must take each case on its merits."[17] Our fullest understanding of any truth comes when we both look at (Contemplate) it and look along (Enjoy) it, bearing in mind that both reason and imagination are involved in the operation of these two modes of seeing.

The relationship between propositional and experiential knowledge, between Contemplation and Enjoyment, between looking at and looking along, is not linear but interactive. These perspectives are necessary aspects of knowing, and every human being naturally shifts between the two. Intellectual understanding can lead to a willingness to enter into a deeper engagement with meaning; an imaginative engagement with the Christian worldview can lead to a desire to seek out, or a willingness to hear, truth expressed in clear propositional form; and the fullest engagement with truth comes from an integrated experience of truth in both modes.

[17] Lewis, "Meditation in a Toolshed," 215.

SEEING

Summer wanes. The heavy-headed roses
Nodding by the river path, the scent
Of sun-warmed earth and hay all mark the closing
Of the year. The warmth was only lent,
And does not last. One morning all is changed:
The hedge is silvered with a sudden frost,
The very paving-stones are furred and strange.
My steps show dark on white where I have crossed
As I set out to walk along the hill.
The winter wind cuts through the leafless trees,
A sharp and sudden cold; my eyes are filled
With water, dazzle-brightning all I see,
In earth and sky: all's silver, gold, and blue,
A sign that spring and summer will come true.

·❖·

CHAPTER TEN

Paradigm Shift

THROUGHOUT this book, I have argued for the value of imagination as part of apologetics—not because the imagination is more important than the reason, or that the arts are more important than philosophy or theology, but because what we most need is *integration*. We need an approach that helps to show the *wholeness* of the Faith. For, after all, we are not merely making a few claims about the world, or about things that happened in the past; we are making a claim about the very nature of reality itself. There is nothing whatsoever in the heavens or the earth or under the earth that is outside our Faith.

Ultimately, the coherence and soundness of Christian teaching (truth), the witness of the Faith lived out faithfully in individual lives, families, and communities (goodness), and the experience of the aesthetic, emotional, and spiritual riches of the liturgy and the arts (beauty) are all connected. Our faith is deeply rooted and fully nourished only if we have all three transcendentals in our lives: goodness, truth, and beauty. Likewise, our apologetics and our evangelization will be most attractive, compelling, and convincing if we draw on all three. Truth, for the intellect; goodness, for the moral sense and the will; beauty, for the aesthetic sense, the emotions, and the imagination. In this way, our apologetics can touch mind, heart, and will, not in isolation, but in harmony with each other.

Certainly, there will always be some people who are most readily helped by apologetics that are based only in philosophical arguments or scriptural claims, or most immediately reached by evangelization that is purely emotional in its attraction. The Holy Spirit is not limited by our limitations. But this does not relieve us of the responsibility to do all that we can with what God has given us, to guide people to knowledge and love of Christ.

An integrated approach to apologetics, one that makes good use of both reason and imagination, will help us greatly.

AN INTEGRATED APPROACH

What do I mean by an integrated approach? We can define it first negatively and then positively. In our work of apologetics, we should *avoid* the following five things:

1) the individualistic approach which divorces the believer from the Church's guidance and fellowship;

2) the rationalistic idea of conversion as *merely* an intellectual decision, or the relativistic idea of conversion as *merely* one particularly appealing narrative among many;

3) the non-sacramental idea of conversion as primarily a personal choice and not a divine gift sealed in baptism;

4) the a-historical idea of conversion as occurring simply and solely at a specific point in time;

5) the militaristic idea that apologetics is a battle that can be somehow 'won' against an unbeliever.

In contrast, an integrated approach that takes full account of imaginative strategies would *include* the following:

1) an emphasis on the individual as part of the Church, guided by her teaching and benefiting from both the fellowship of contemporary fellow believers and the examples provided by, and the communion available with, the saints in heaven;

2) a recognition of reason, imagination, and the will, all as equally important faculties of the human person;

3) a constant awareness of the work of the Holy Spirit and of the value of grace given through the sacraments, as the primary and most important aspect of conversion;

4) an appreciation of conversion as a process occurring in time and space, one that cannot be forced

or rushed, though it can and should be facilitated and encouraged;

5) a fundamental grounding of all apologetics work in the virtue of *love*, seeing the unbeliever rightly, as beloved by God, and a future brother or sister in Christ.

Done well, apologetics places rational argument firmly in the incarnational reality of the Faith as it is lived out and experienced in the sacraments, prayer, fellowship, worship, and service, and it engages the imagination and emotions as well as the intellect. Eucharistic worship and the witness of the saints offer examples of this union of rational and imaginative ways of knowing, and thus can guide us in the attempt to develop the imaginative approach to apologetics as it needs to be developed to properly complement the propositional mode.

To begin with, consider one of the deepest underlying issues in apologetics: the question of epistemic security. How do we *know* that we are right? The skeptic may well argue that it is impossible to attain complete certainty about the things that Christians hold to be true. Can we conclusively demonstrate that God exists, that Jesus rose from the dead, that we who are baptized are temples of the Holy Spirit, that those who have died in friendship with Christ have eternal life, that Scripture is completely without error, and so on? In one sense, no, we cannot *prove* these claims, however strong our evidence and arguments may be. For every argument that we advance—whether logical, evidential, or historical—the skeptic can always offer an alternative explanation, or simply hold out the theoretical possibility of an alternate explanation. This need not make us uneasy. For one thing, as we discussed in our chapter on doubt, in our ordinary lives we are accustomed to making all sorts of important decisions without complete certainty, based on a reasonable judgment of the evidence at hand. Furthermore, we can concede to our skeptical friend that we cannot achieve *certainty* on these sorts of questions by the use of reason *alone*—but we need not accept the premise that this is the only way to attain firm knowledge of the truth!

In particular, the Catholic recognizes that the individual is part of the Church, and that the Church, established by Our Lord Jesus Christ himself and guided by the Holy Spirit, is *supernaturally grounded* in truth. Jesus's claim to be the Son of God was vindicated by his Resurrection from the dead: an event in history. Likewise, Jesus's granting of authority to the apostles, and the coming of the Holy Spirit at Pentecost (the 'birthday of the Church'), were events in history. The reality of these events, and of the consequences that flow from them, is not dependent on the interpretation or understanding of the individual believer.

As Catholics, as part of the Church founded by Jesus himself, we are organically (not metaphorically) united with Christ as his Bride. Thus, in accepting the teaching of the Church and, above all, in participating in the sacraments, the individual finds the epistemically secure position that cannot be achieved by individual intellect alone.

In the Eucharist we encounter Christ fully and experientially; our encounter with him is not un-reasonable, but it is also not dependent on human reason, nor is it limited by our ability to describe, analyze, or understand it. In all the sacraments, we have the objective certainty of the gift of grace through the Holy Spirit; in the Eucharist, as in the Incarnation, human reason can tell us certain things about the experience, without ever exhausting the reality of the One whom we encounter. Thus, we have the grounding to be objectively certain of the Truth whom we encounter, even while being keenly aware of our own limitations in communicating about that Truth. Nowhere is this more profoundly illustrated than in the witness of the saints and, above all, the martyrs.

From the earliest days of the Church, Christians have honored the martyrs, those who witnessed to their faith with their blood. This witness was convincing: as Tertullian said, the blood of the martyrs is the seed of the Church. The Christian martyrs testify *both* from personal conviction (as does a martyr for any cause) *and* from an epistemically secure position regarding the Truth, even if they are unable objectively to demonstrate it. Their witness is ultimately grounded not on their own knowledge or intellectual capacities, but on the Church, the "pillar and bulwark of the truth."[1]

Consider Bl. Humphrey Pritchard, one of the Oxford Martyrs of the sixteenth century. Pritchard, a serving-man at an Oxford inn, was arrested along with the innkeeper and the two recusant priests they were hiding. All were condemned to death and, on July 5, 1589, were hanged. When Pritchard was brought to the scaffold, an

---

[1] 1 Timothy 3:15.

Anglican priest in the crowd mocked him by saying that, though he was dying for being a Catholic, he could not even explain what being a Catholic means. Pritchard retorted: "Though I may not be able to tell you in words what it means to be a Catholic, God knows my heart, and he knows that I believe all that the Holy Roman Church believes, and that which I am unable to explain in words I am here to explain and attest with my blood."[2]

Pritchard's apologetic was his death as a martyr. It was an 'enacted apologetic,' if you like: concrete, real, substantial, not merely verbal. Though Pritchard lacked the words to make a case for his Catholic faith, he did not need them: his life and the manner of his death spoke more articulately than any amount of doctrinal exposition ever could.

Not that there is anything wrong with verbal presentations of the Faith. And indeed, Pritchard's witness is part of a larger community, one that includes the intellectual apologetics work of monumental figures like St. Thomas Aquinas, Bl. John Henry Cardinal Newman, and Pope Benedict XVI.

We need arguments, art, and personal witness. The ear cannot say to the hand or the eye, "I have no need of you"[3]: so, too, the apologist cannot say to the martyr, "I have my arguments; I have no need of your witness"—nor to the poet, the filmmaker, the shelter volunteer, the mother of children, "I have my arguments; I have no need of your art, or your service, or your love."

---

[2] Fr. Leon Pereira, O.P., "Catholic Martyrs of Oxford" (Blackfriars, Oxford: 2000), 3. See also Alban Butler, *Butler's Lives of the Saints, vol. 7* (Collegeville, MN: The Liturgical Press, 2000), 39.

[3] 1 Corinthians 12:21.

Christian faith includes assent to propositions, but it is more than just a set of propositions; it is an entirely different way of looking at and living in the world. The experience of turning from unbelief to belief involves a tectonic shift in values and identity; depending on the particular individual's prior beliefs, becoming convinced of the truth of Christianity may involve a terrifying dislocation of familiar ideas, the relinquishment of convictions previously held as basic truth, and a turn to an entirely new and existentially demanding way of being in the world.

With the dramatic nature of this shift in mind, we can better appreciate that propositional knowledge about Christianity, though necessary, may not be sufficient to help a nonbeliever make the action of the will necessary to accept Christ as Savior. More is needed. As Alison Milbank argues, "in apologetics we do not just want to convince people of the rationality of what we believe as if it were a fact about the population of the Galapagos Islands: we want to make them understand in a *participatory* way."[4] Or, to put it in Bl. John Henry Newman's terms, we want to help people move from inference to assent, and for that assent to be real, not merely notional and abstract. The fact of the Resurrection, and its implications, can be understood by the reason, but it is imagination that helps establish its meaning—and thereby makes it a real, living, life-changing idea.

---

[4] Alison Milbank, "Apologetics and the Imagination: Making Strange," in *Imaginative Apologetics: Theology, Philosophy, and the Catholic Tradition*, ed. Andrew Davison (Grand Rapids, MI: Baker Academic, 2011), 32.

BOTH/AND

As we saw in the previous chapter, we need both Contemplation and Enjoyment in our apologetics efforts. It is worth remembering, as Lewis shows us, that we cannot Enjoy something *at the same time* that we Contemplate it. To begin to Contemplate (to look 'at') something takes us instantly out of Enjoying it (looking 'along' it). Because we are at every moment sustained by God, the Ground of All Being, no one can look 'at' God from an entirely neutral, outside perspective: to do so would be to take ourselves out of existence entirely, for "in him we live and move and have our being."[5] In a sense, then, it is not possible to Contemplate God, only to Enjoy him, by the very act of existing—whether or not we recognize what it is that we are doing. Likewise, in one sense, Christians can never look 'at' the Faith as something outside ourselves, because we are now temples of the Holy Spirit, and cannot separate ourselves from him. We are always looking 'along' the Spirit.[6]

Yet, paradoxically, because we are made in the image of God, we can in a sense exercise Contemplation even in the midst of Enjoyment. God has so made us that we, using the twin faculties of imagination and reason, can think meaningful thoughts *about* him, even while we as thinking beings are sustained in existence *by* him. Likewise, we can to a certain extent Enjoy perspectives that do not overlap with our own, by the exercise of imaginative

---

[5] Acts 17:28.
[6] I am indebted to Michael Ward, and in particular for his work on *Surprised by Joy*, for the insights in this section.

sympathy. We are like birds in flight, knowing that we are upheld by air currents that we cannot see; and though we cannot live beneath the waters, we can yet recognize that there is a deep-sea realm and even imagine what it is like to breathe water as a fish. This ability to Contemplate what we Enjoy makes it possible for us to understand our Faith more fully and deeply, and thus discern what will help others to see the truth that sustains us all.

Arguments are always necessary, in order to correct the errors and omissions of the day. As Lewis put it, "Good philosophy must exist, if for no other reason, because bad philosophy needs to be answered."[7] The specific form that these arguments take, and the specific topics that the apologist must address, will vary in different contexts, and the Church's teaching must be made clear in fresh language and examples to each generation. So, too, with imaginative apologetics. We must be attentive to help people see the beauty of the Faith, to enter into its wonder and joy; to see afresh; to find the Faith meaningful, so that they may discover it to be true.

We need both propositional argument and imaginative engagement, continually shaped and re-shaped to show the truth in fresh ways. The Faith can never be reduced to a single knockout argument that will be convincing for all who hear it, or a single knockout work of art that will be transformative for all who see it—nor should we wish for such a thing, for it would be tantamount to saying that we don't need the Holy Spirit. It is the Holy Spirit who

---

[7] C. S. Lewis, "Learning in War-Time," in *The Weight of Glory and Other Addresses* (New York: HarperCollins, 2001), 58.

brings conviction. Though we should labor with all our might to develop both abstract and the concrete presentations of the Faith, we must remember that, however much we may plant and water, it is God who gives the growth.

But even more than that, the Faith can never be reduced to a single argument, or a single image, because it is a living thing. When we invite people to enter into the Church, we are inviting them to come home and, in so doing, also to explore a glorious new country, where there is always more to discover. We are inviting them to be made truly whole, as unique individuals, and also to discover the joyous fellowship of the communion of the saints, living and dead.

This is the vision we must try, as best we can, to share: that the universe is profoundly meaningful, that all things are interconnected in and through Christ, and that to be a Christian is to be fully alive, now and eternally. God is the ultimate Artist, and Author, and Composer: in his work, all creation sings, and each of us is called to join in the cosmic harmony.

PARADIGM SHIFT: ANGELUS

Within the deepest silence is a sound:
Ordered, graceful, the music of the spheres
Reverberates in every atom, bounds
From star to star: a song we cannot hear,
Except in hints and glimpses: in the hush
Of twilight, crickets with their tiny words;
A smile upon a sleeping face; a rush
Of love within the heart; high circling birds
Against the burning blue of heaven; sparrows
Darting quick into the hedge; the air before
The rain and after; mossy bridges, furrows
At harvest: woven, a vast cosmic score
In secret sung. And we beneath the moon
Can add our prayers: sunset, sunrise, noon.

Recommended Reading

Barfield, Owen, *Poetic Diction: A Study in Meaning* (Middletown, Connecticut: Wesleyan University Press, 1973).

Begbie, Jeremy (ed.), *Beholding the Glory: Incarnation through the Arts* (Grand Rapids, MI: Baker Academic, 2001).

Chesterton, G. K., *Orthodoxy* (Chicago: Moody Publishers, 2009); first published 1908.

Davison, Andrew (ed.), *Imaginative Apologetics: Theology, Philosophy, and the Catholic Tradition* (Grand Rapids, MI: Baker Academic, 2011).

Gabelman, Josephine, *A Theology of Nonsense* (Eugene, OR: Wipf and Stock, 2016).

Gioia, Dana, *The Catholic Writer Today* (Newberg, OR: Wiseblood Books, 2014).

Guite, Malcolm, *Faith, Hope and Poetry: Theology and the Poetic Imagination* (Farnham, Surrey: Ashgate, 2010).

———. "Telling the Truth through Imaginative Fiction," in *C. S. Lewis at Poets' Corner*, ed. Michael Ward and Peter S. Williams (Eugene, OR: Cascade Books, 2016).

Lewis, C. S., *The Abolition of Man: A Critical Edition by Michael Ward*, ed. Michael Ward (Chicago: Teller Books, 2017).

————. "Bluspels and Flalansferes: A Semantic Nightmare," in *Selected Literary Essays,* ed. Walter Hooper (Cambridge: Cambridge University Press, 1969).

————. "Meditation in a Toolshed," in *God in the Dock: Essays on Theology and Ethics,* ed. Walter Hooper (Grand Rapids, MI: William B. Eerdmans, 1970).

————. "On Stories" and "Sometimes Fairy Stories May Say Best What's to Be Said," in *On Stories and Other Essays on Literature,* ed. Walter Hooper (Orlando: Harcourt, 1966).

MacDonald, George, "The Imagination: Its Functions and Its Culture" and "The Fantastic Imagination," in *A Dish of Orts: Chiefly Papers on the Imagination, and on Shakespeare*: available at: <http://www.gutenberg.org/ebooks/9393>.

Newman, Bl. John Henry Cardinal, *An Essay in Aid of a Grammar of Assent* (Assumption Press, 2013); first published 1870.

Ordway, Holly, *Not God's Type: An Atheist Academic Lays Down Her Arms* (San Francisco: Ignatius Press, 2014).

Sayers, Dorothy L., *The Mind of the Maker* (New York: HarperCollins, 1979); first published 1941.

Talliaferro, Charles and Jil Evans, *The Image in Mind: Theism, Naturalism, and the Imagination* (New York: Continuum, 2011).

Tolkien, J. R. R., "On Fairy-stories," in *Tolkien On Fairy-stories: Expanded edition, with commentary and notes*, ed. Verlyn Flieger and Douglas A. Anderson (London: HarperCollins, 2014).

Topping, Ryan S., *Rebuilding Catholic Culture: How the Catechism Can Shape Our Common Life* (Manchester, NH: Sophia Institute Press, 2012).

Ward, Michael, "Introduction" and "Commentary," *The Abolition of Man: A Critical Edition by Michael Ward*, by C. S. Lewis, ed. Michael Ward (Chicago: Teller Books, 2017).

———. "The Good Serves the Better and Both the Best: C. S. Lewis on Imagination and Reason in Apologetics," in *Imaginative Apologetics: Theology, Philosophy, and the Catholic Tradition*, ed. Andrew Davison (Grand Rapids, MI: Baker Academic, 2011).

———. *Planet Narnia: The Seven Heavens in the Imagination of C. S. Lewis* (Oxford: Oxford University Press, 2008).

ACKNOWLEDGMENTS

My thanks go first of all to Fr. David Meconi, for commissioning this book, and to Carl Olson for suggesting it. I would like also to thank my editor, Chris Erickson, for his gracious assistance on this project.

The material in this book has taken shape over the past six or eight years, as I have written, taught, and lectured on literature and imaginative apologetics in many different venues. The questions and comments from attendees at my lectures have been very helpful both in showing me the need for a book specifically on imaginative apologetics and in providing insight into what topics to include.

In particular, I appreciate the opportunity to give the Strauss Lectures at Lincoln Christian University, and to speak on this topic for many different universities, organizations, churches, and conferences, including Auburn University, Northwest University, Southwest Baptist University, Dallas Baptist University, Regent University, the Reasons Conference in The Woodlands, TX, the Thrive Conference in Sacramento, CA, Athanatos Christian Ministries, Reasons to Believe in Houston, TX, the Bible & Beer Fellowship, the Evangelical Philosophical Society Apologetics Conference, St. Michael Catholic Church in Houston, TX, and the C. S. Lewis Foundation Summer Institute in Oxford, England.

I also wish to thank *Transpositions*, the online journal of the Institute for Theology in the Arts at the University of St. Andrews; the *Novel Thoughts* blog of Ignatius Press; *The City* journal of Houston Baptist University; and the *Christian Research Journal*, for the opportunity to test-drive some of my thoughts about imaginative apologetics in articles for them.

Thanks also go to my students in the M.A. in Apologetics program at Houston Baptist University, particularly my Cultural Apologetics students, whose response to these ideas in my teaching has been stimulating.

My appreciative thanks to Michael Ward, whose insightful comments and suggestions on the draft of this book made it vastly better in both prose and poetry.

Finally, my sincere thanks to Malcolm Guite, not only for the kind permission to use his sonnet "O Clavis," but, more broadly, for the implicit 'call to arms' to further develop imaginative apologetics that he issued in his marvelous study, *Faith, Hope and Poetry: Theology and the Poetic Imagination*. Malcolm combines the ability to analyze imaginative apologetics with the ability to practice it through poetry and song. I dedicate this book to him with gratitude and respect.

La Crosse, Wisconsin
8th December 2016

Index

A

abortion, see life issues

anthropomorphization, 50

apologetics, 1–2, 11–13, 149, 170

argument from desire, 133–135

Aristotle, 16

architecture, 129–130, 142–146

art, 41, 100, 129–130, 145–146, 167

Aslan, see Lewis

atheism, 3, 9, 89, 109, 134, 137–138

Aquinas, St. Thomas, 16, 173

Augustine, St., 16

Austen, Jane, 33, 109, 109n8

authority, 151–155

autonomy, 62, 64n3, 67–68, 152–155

B

Barfield, Owen, 17, 46–47, 60–61, 80–81, 179

Barnes, Marc, 70n8, 156–159

beauty, 11, 114, 129, 131–132, 142–146, 149, 167–168, 176

Begbie, Jeremy, 179

Benedict XVI, Pope, 173

Benson, Robert Hugh, 155n5

Bonaventure, St., 16

I

imaginative apologetics,
    challenges for, 152–155
    definition of, 15
    emotions in, 101–102
    incarnational element of, 98–108, 160, 170
    narrative in, 102–106
    role of, 149
    specificity in, 106–108
imagination,
    definition of, 15–16, 149
    failure of, 150–151
    functioning of, 16–18, 88–90, 149–150
    limitations of, 155
    and theory of mind, 109
    relationship with reason, 10–11, 15–19, 29, 57, 85,
        87–88, 149–150, 160–161, 164, 167–169, 174–176
Incarnation, the, 83, 97–99, 141
integration, 85–86, 160–164, 167–177

J

Jesus, 3–4, 10–11, 22–24, 46, 54–56, 77, 88, 90, 92–93,
    97–100, 101, 104, 107–108, 116–117, 119, 123, 143,
    153–154, 170–171
John Paul II, Pope St., 69
Joy, 105, 125, 130, 139–142

L

language,
    distortion of, 27–28, 59–61 68–71
    emotional impact of, 72–75, 101–102